Making it Alone

**A study of the care experiences
of young black people**

Lynda Ince

B *r i t i s h*
A *g e n c i e s*
f o r **A** *d o p t i o n*
a n d **F** *o s t e r i n g*

Published by
British Agencies for Adoption & Fostering
(BAAF)
Skyline House
200 Union Street
London SE1 0LX

Charity registration 275689

© Lynda Ince 1998

British Library Cataloguing in Publication Data
A catalogue record for this book is available
from the British Library

ISBN 1 873868 51 0

Designed by Andrew Haig & Associates
Typeset by Avon Dataset Ltd, Bidford on
Avon, Warwickshire B50 4JH
Printed by Russell Press (TU), Nottingham

Acknowledgements

Sincere thanks and acknowledgements are expressed to all the young people who willingly consented to participating in this study, giving unsparingly of their time and sharing their personal experiences. I trust that this research will accurately and sensitively reflect the strength of feeling that was communicated in the interviews with them. It is my sincere hope the publication of this book will bring about change for black children in care and young black people leaving care.

I wish to acknowledge my family for their solid support in a number of ways throughout the duration of the M Phil course, in particular, my mother Mrs. Oxley, my son Michael, my brother Daryl Oxley and sisters, Deniece Oxley, Dr. Gozil Oxley, Judy Oxley, Joy Oxley and Pauline Straughn.

I have very much appreciated the support of my fellow student and friend Vince White, and Penny Youll of Brunel University. Finally, thanks to June Thoburn (University of East Anglia) and Paul Macey (Black Perspectives Advisory Committee, BAAF) for commenting on earlier drafts of the script, and to Shaila Shah, Head of Communications at BAAF, whose advice and editorial input have been invaluable.

This book is dedicated to my mother and my son.

The author

Lynda Ince is a part-time lecturer on the Diploma in Social Work course at North Hertfordshire College and also works for the London Borough of Harrow as an Independent Reviewing Officer. She completed her M Phil at Brunel University of West London, the outcome of which is this publication. Lynda became a social worker in 1982, and specialised in working with children and families. For nine years she held the position of a senior social worker and then as manager, Children and Families.

Glossary

BLACK

This is a political term that is used to refer to individuals or groups who originate from or are descendants of people from Africa, the Caribbean and the Indian Subcontinent, and are distinguished by the colour of their skin. All have a shared history of oppression that is based on economics and power relations. The term black includes children of mixed heritage where one parent is black.

CULTURE

A body of learned behaviour that is transmitted through individuals and communities. It is based on factors such as traditions, memories, family attitudes, class, money, status, division of family roles.

DISCRIMINATION

Showing partiality in treatment. The practice that treats people unequally.

MINORITY ETHNIC GROUP

Belonging to a cultural, racial or religious group that is numerically smaller that the majority group.

ETHNOCENTRISM

The attitude that one's own ethnic group, nation or culture is superior to all others.

IDENTITY

Definition or concept of self in relation to others.

IN CARE

This term is used in this book in preference to the more recent terminology following the Children Act 1989 of "looked after" and "accommodated" children. It includes long-term and short-term foster and residential care.

MIXED HERITAGE

A child that is born to parents of whom one is black and one is white.

PRIVATE FOSTERING

A private arrangement made by parents for care to be administered to a child by substitute carers. The majority of privately fostered children are of West African origin and most commonly, their carers are white.

RACE

Categorisation of people, historically constructed by notions of superiority and inferiority.

RACISM

Belief in the inherent superiority of one race. Individual racism stems from the beliefs and actions of a single person. Institutional racism includes that of establishments, organisations of legal systems and customs having a social, educational, political, economic or religious function.

RACIAL IDENTITY
A concept of self in relation to others based on one's racial and cultural heritage.

SAME RACE PLACEMENTS
A term used to describe the placement of children with substitute families who are of the same race or cultural background.

TRANSRACIAL
The practice of placing black children in adoptive or foster homes with white substitute carers.

Contents

Foreword

The continual onslaught of racial disadvantage and discrimination in employment, education, housing, health and social welfare has a devastating effect upon the life chances of minority ethnic families and their children. Issues of power and domination intertwined with race, class, and gender have a considerable impact upon the structural position of minority groups. Over the last few decades, the response of the personal social services to deal adequately with the needs and concerns of minority families and children has proved to be wanting.

My own research into race and the child welfare system over the last ten years has revealed that the two groups most affected are the children of African-Caribbean and inter-racial families. The experiences of South Asian families are also beginning to be documented.

The high representation of African-Caribbean and mixed-parentage children in the care system is worrying. Their precipitous entry into care and lengthy periods of stay in the care system require serious and urgent attention on the quality of early intervention in the lives of these families. We know that mixed-parentage children in care come from families where the carer is their white birth mother. The vulnerability of such children and the needs and concerns of their mothers have, hitherto, received little recognition in the fields of social work research and practice.

Although we have some understanding of the entry and placement situation of minority ethnic children in the care system, little is known about their subjective experiences of being looked after by local authority social services. Lynda Ince's study of ten black youngsters' experiences of long-term care and leaving care is a welcome addition to the slowly growing literature in this area. Whilst Ince's study sample is small, it does offer a unique insight into the care experiences of these youngsters and paves the way for further research in this area.

Previous research on care leavers has highlighted issues around isolation, loneliness, homelessness, unemployment, poor education, and lack of information. Lynda Ince's study shows that the experiences of black care leavers are further heightened by direct and indirect discrimination which compounds the above problems. Ince draws our attention to aspects documented by previous research that black children enter care at an early age and remain in care for lengthy periods. The pervading effects of lengthy periods in care upon young people's self-image, particularly in terms of their ethnic and cultural identity, are stressed. Loss of contact with birth parents and the black community adds to these problems. Ince found that the majority of young people in her study grew up with little or no knowledge of their ethnic and cultural heritage.

Ince also signifies the importance of direct work with black children in the care system. Such work is crucial to help fill the gaps in young people's understanding about their situation. Indeed the youngsters' feelings of loss, sadness and rejection are intensified by displacement from their racial and cultural grouping. Moreover, Ince shows that the racial and cultural vacuum created by transracial placements leads to internalised racism in black young people. Such circumstances make it essential for appropriate direct social work to take place.

The problems of minority ethnic families and children and the failure of the child welfare system to deal with these adequately requires open and explicit discussion. Needless to say, further research is required to explore the circumstances of black families who come to the attention of social services for help and assistance. The existing knowledge base, grounded in original empirical research, in this area should be utilised by social services managers and practitioners in the formulation and delivery of adequate and appropriate service provision to black families and children.

Ravinder Barn
Senior Lecturer in Applied Social Studies
Royal Holloway, University of London

Introduction

Black children make up a relatively small percentage of the total population in Britain today, yet there has been much concern about their over-representation in the public care system. A statistical report based on the 1991 census data on the ethnic composition of the population and published by the Commission for Racial Equality (CRE)[1] shows a variation between minority ethnic populations on the basis of age, with some minority ethnic groups being more highly represented in the younger age range of the population. The table below shows age ranges of different ethnic groups in percentages with particular reference to groups relevant to this study. This information is of vital importance for the strategic planning of children's services.

	Total Population	0–4 %	5–15 %	16–24 %
White	51,873.8	6.36	12.97	12.55
Black	809.7	11.2	18.28	16.11
Black Caribbean	500.0	7.56	14.33	14.87
Black African	212.4	11.83	17.51	16.61
Black Other	178.4	20.28	30.27	19.01

Table 1

Ethnic groups in Britain with reference to ages

Note: These figures have been obtained from OPCS

Black children in care

The paucity of statistical data and the absence of established systems for monitoring the black looked after children population makes it extremely difficult to establish accurate numbers of black children entering and leaving the care system. As far back as 1984, the House of Commons Social Services Committee[2] acknowledged that it was impossible to plan for and meet the needs of black and minority ethnic children 'if the simplest facts are not available'. A research study[3] commissioned by the CRE and published by British Agencies for Adoption and Fostering (BAAF) in 1997 reinforced this. Further, a recommendation that central government take a lead in ethnic monitoring by requiring local authorities to supply information on the ethnicity, religion and language of children in receipt of social services was strongly made.

Research studies[4,5,6] published in the late 1980s and early 90s are only just beginning to offer a picture of patterns of entry into care: these demonstrate that black children, particularly African-Caribbean and African, have been over-represented while Asian children are under-represented in all age groups. Among adolescents only African-Caribbean youth entered care at a slightly higher rate than white youth. Rowe et al[7] in 1989 also found differences between minority ethnic groups, with African-Caribbean and African children being highly represented in the preschool 5–10 age group, twice the number entering the care system compared with their white counterparts. The most striking finding of that same study was that the group most at risk of entering care were black children of mixed heritage. The authors reported high admission and multiple admission rates for this group, more than twice that of white children. Black children of mixed heritage were also highly represented in the preschool age range and also more likely to be on care orders in all age categories. These concerns were reiterated by Bebbington and Miles[8] and very recently by Barn et al.[9]

Reasons for black children coming into care

The reasons for the referral and entry of black children into the care system have been and continue to be complex, and cannot be understood outside the context of wider social and economic factors including poor housing, inequality in access to educational opportunities and employment and, in general, institutional and individual racism. In the absence of documented evidence, the CRE[10] speculated in 1978 that some of the major causes for black children entering the care system were associated with cultural differences, stressful home conditions related to the aforementioned factors, single parenthood and lack of appropriate services to meet need. Black children also come into the care system because they have suffered abuse, and in such cases, social workers have a duty to protect them without allowing cultural differences to lead to differential and unequal treatment, thereby placing children at even greater risk because of their "race" or culture.

Thus social work intervention with black children must be seen in the context of the complex dynamics of racism and institutional practices. To overlook the "race" dimension is to ignore the prime reason for misassessment and flawed judgement that can often lead to over-intrusive approaches resulting in a disproportionate number of black children in local authority care.

Experiences in care

A child's entry into care is the beginning of an experience that may last for many years, and, in some cases, all of a child's growing life. Professionals and carers take on the role of parents and, by virtue of that position, become the most significant "others" in the child's life. Yet, very little is known about how black children and young people interpret this experience and give it meaning. The lack of authoritative and dependable research has contributed to a lack of understanding about black children's experiences in care. The literature review shows that research on black children in care has not developed in line with the numbers of black children in the care system. It also shows the low level of preparation young people receive for independent living after spending a substantial period of their lives in care. Many professionals consequently remain unaware of the true effects of the care experience on young black people. Ahmad[11] stated that it is the lack of research within the social work profession that has largely led to the needs of black children remaining 'unidentified and unmet'.

Although change has been slow, nevertheless some strides have been made to acknowledge the contributions of black professionals in advising about the needs of black children in care. Small,[12] Divine,[13] Cheetham[14] and ABSWAP[15] have made a very valuable contribution to the discourse on transracial placements. The work of Ahmad[16] has been significant in commenting on the welfare of black children and their families.

The Children Act 1989 for the first time in England and Wales gave the key message that decisions about children must give due attention to race, culture, language and religion. The Children (Scotland) Act 1995, too, stipulates this. Local authorities have also been urged to recruit foster and day carers that would reflect different ethnic groups in the community, thus reflecting the needs of children needing placements.

The Central Council for Education and Training in Social Work[17] in recognising the multicultural context of Britain acknowledged that the 'placement of black children in rural children's homes and foster settings in the 1950s and 1960s made race an operational issue for social work organisation'. It argued that the solitary black child in a rural authority was exposed to the same level of oppression 'as if he/she lived anywhere else'. Thus in more recent years, the promotion of anti-discriminatory practice was high on the agenda in training for social workers, encouraging an important shift in promoting anti-racist and anti-oppressive practice and focusing on diversity and difference.

Brief description of the research

This is a qualitative in-depth study of young black people's experience of long-term care in two local authorities in England. It is exploratory and descriptive and provides an understanding of the experiences of black young people in care and leaving care. The study addresses the distinctive nature of the young people's experiences in direct relation to their "race" and culture, investigating the impact of their care experience on racial and cultural identity. It also examines the level of preparation for leaving care, and considers the extent to which "race", culture and identity have been acknowledged by professionals as an integral part of growth and development. All of the young people in this study had been placed in long-term care in the early 1970s.

The sample consists of ten young black people who had either left care or who were in the process of doing so at the time this study was conducted. The interviews were supplemented by interviews with two senior professionals in the two local authorities from which the samples were taken.

The structure of the study

The report begins by setting the context against which social services provision for black children has been made in Britain. It offers a discussion of relevant legislation – child care and immigration – and its particular impact on young black children in the care system. Chapter 2 explores relevant themes in the literature on leaving care with particular reference to that which exists on young black people leaving care while Chapter 3 examines the concepts of "race", culture and identity. Chapter 4 describes the research study and Chapter 5 begins by offering pen portraits of the study sample. The following chapters provide the findings. A concluding chapter discusses the prominent themes that emerge.

Terminology

Throughout this report, the term "black" is used to refer to minority ethnic groups in general, but principally to those of African and African-Caribbean origin as well as those of mixed heritage.

The term "in care" has been used to broadly describe both foster care and residential care, short-term and long-term. Although this term has been replaced by the term "looked after" since the Children Act 1989 it was deemed more appropriate to use "in care" as the experiences of the study sample mostly predate the 1989 Act.

References

1   Centre for Research in Ethnic Minorities in Great Britain, Census Statistical Paper No. 2, *Age and Gender Structure*, ESCR and CRE, 1993.
2   Social Services Inspectorate, *Inspection of Community Homes*, DoH, 1985.
3   Barn R, Sinclair R, and Ferdinand D, *Acting on Principle: An examination of race and ethnicity in social services provision for children and families*, BAAF, 1997.
4   Barn R, *Black Children in the Public Care System*, BAAF/Batsford, 1993.
5   Department of Health, *Patterns and Outcomes in Child Placement: Messages from current research and their implications*, HMSO, 1991.
6   Rowe J, Hundleby M and Garnett L, *Child Care Now: A survey of placement patterns*, BAAF, 1989.
7   See 6 above.
8   Bebbington A and Miles J, "The background of children who enter local authority care", *British Journal of Social Work*, 19:5, 349–368, 1989.
9   See 3 above.
10 Commission for Racial Equality, *Multi-Racial Britain: The social services response – A Working Party Report*, CRE, 1978.
11 Ahmad A, *Services to Black People*, Race Equality Unit, 1988.
12 Small J, "Transracial placements: conflicts and contradictions," in Ahmed S, Cheetham J and Small J, *Social Work with Black Children and their Families*, BAAF/Batsford, 1986.
13 Divine D, "No problems," *Caribbean Times*, 4 March 1983.
14 Cheetham J, "Reviewing black children in care," in Ahmed S, Cheetham J and Small J, *Social Work with Black Children and their Families*, BAAF/Batsford, 1986.
15 Association of Black Social Workers and Allied Professions, *Black Children in Care, Evidence to the House of Commons Social Services Committee*, 1983.
16 Ahmad B, *Black Perspectives in Social Work*, BASW, 1992.
17 Central Council for Education and Training in Social Work, *One Step Towards Racial Justice*, Pluto Press, 1992.

Setting the context

It is important to set this study in context by considering the role of legislation in shaping policy development and professional practice. This chapter focuses on the development of child care legislation (in England and Wales) but also includes immigration and race relations legislation and assesses the ways in which all these have responded to the needs of black children.

CHILD CARE LEGISLATION

Since 1948, legislation has reinforced the paramount interests of the child. The Children Act 1948 established the roots of the personal social services through the introduction of children's departments. It was also an important landmark for introducing a professional approach to the care of children who were "deprived". A Home Office circular[1] had stipulated that the first aim of the Act was to keep the family together, and that the separation of a child from his or her parents could only be justified when there was no possibility of securing adequate care within the family. This guiding principle, embedded in the very early legislation, raises fundamental questions as to why black children have continued to remain in long-term local authority care and why welfare and preventive services have not been forthcoming for black families.

The Children Act 1948

The Children Act 1948 emerged as a result of a recognition of the conditions of poverty in which young children were being nurtured. The conditions for admission into care were set out in section 1 of the Act and stated that a child could be admitted to care if abandoned by parents or guardian, or because the parents (owing to illness or disease) were incapable of caring for the child, or that the intervention of the local authority was necessary to protect the interests and welfare of the child. It was deemed important that admission to care should normally be at the request of parents and that a child should not be detained in care any longer than was necessary, provided this was consistent with the child's welfare. New insights into the needs of children emerged with the setting up of children's services, one of the most important being to consider the individual needs of children and their families.

1950–1960

The 1950s saw a general improvement in economic conditions and a growing awareness of the complex needs of children in public care. Of particular significance were the recommendations of the Curtis Committee which advised that ratios of staff to children should be 1:10 in children's homes. Some social services departments appointed specialist adoption workers and area offices were set up, thus enabling easier access to services and encouraging local neighbourhood services to be developed. The latter years of the 1950s saw some creative and pioneering work and a drive towards greater understanding of the need for methodical inquiry and a more professional approach to intervention. Change was also facilitated by Bowlby's[2] research on maternal deprivation and was influential in encouraging a shift away from residential care for children. There was debate and controversy about the importance of family and biological blood ties. In 1954, the Hurst Committee[3] pointed out that the welfare of the child was of primary importance and that adoption should be a means of satisfying the need of the *child* as opposed to those of the adopters. It is important to note that, from this very early stage, there was concern that to give paramount consideration to the welfare of the child could lead to situations where parents requesting temporary care might lose their children.

The significance for black children

During the early years of policy formation very little reference was made to "race" even though there had been significant state intervention based on the recognition that those who needed assistance were not to be treated as a residual minority. This was underpinned by notions of universalism and the need for all sections of the community to utilise services which would be provided in exactly the same way for both the majority and minority populations. However, Williams'[4] critique of the developing welfare state showed that policies had been shaped by notions of family and nation in which there was no analysis of "race" or gender. The Beveridge Report[5] was couched in terms of maintaining British values at a time when cheap labour was imported from the Commonwealth to resolve work force problems, but immigrant families had little or no access to personal social services.

1960–1970

During this decade, the growing awareness of the need to protect children was given significant priority. The Ingleby Committee[6] was set up to consider the operation of the juvenile courts, the prevention of cruelty to children, and issues of "moral danger". The question under consideration was whether local authorities should be given stronger powers to prevent the suffering of children through neglect in their homes.

The Children and Young Persons Act 1963

The Children and Young Persons Act 1963 was an outcome of the Ingleby Report which stressed the importance of service delivery in terms of extending availability and accessibility of social services. Pringle and Naidoo[7] emphasised the importance of preventive work with children and families and for help and advice to be readily available from the local authority, thereby reducing the need to receive or keep children in care or to bring them before the juvenile court. The 1963 Act was important because for the first time it defined help in terms of financial assistance to be offered to promote the welfare of the child. The Act was also responsible for varying the grounds under which the local authority could assume parental rights for a child in care under section 2 of the 1948 Children Act.

The Seebhom Report

In 1968, the report of the Seebohm Committee[8] made a number of recommendations aimed at resolving organisational problems in the provision and co-ordination of services including those for young children. Among these was the establishment of unified social services. These recommendations were embodied in the Local Authorities Social Services Act and became law in 1970, thereby abolishing local authority children's departments and the creation of the Personal Social Services in 1970 under the Director of Social Services. In essence these changes led to the specialisation of social work which radically altered provision of services.

The Children and Young Persons Act 1969

The focus of the Children and Young Persons Act 1969 (section 1) was its concern with children brought before the juvenile courts. Under this Act a number of conditions had to be satisfied before the courts could make an order including the importance of establishing that all other alternatives were exhausted, and that an order would ensure that the child was given the care and control needed. The Act gave a new duty to local authorities to advise, guide and assist families by offering a range of preventive services with the objective of avoiding situations of risk by making services accessible. Nevertheless, by 1990, 36.7 per cent (22,231) of all children in care were under orders made under the 1969 Act. (This must be seen against the growing trend between 1980 and 1990 of a decrease in the total number of children entering care, accounted for by a fall of 11 per cent in the population of children/young people.)

The significance for black children

An important aspect of the 1969 Act was the creation of Community Homes with Education on the premises (CHEs) which the local authority managed and controlled; the authority had the option of offering a CHE as accommodation for a child in care. However, this had adverse effects on black children – research by Lambert[9] in Birmingham showed that CHE accommodation was used excessively for black children. A study by Pearce[10] of 125 approved schools echoed this finding and concluded that African-Caribbean boys were more likely to be found in this type of local authority care. High levels of contact with the police were also cause for concern. The juvenile police liaison scheme proposed close co-operation between the police and social services to avoid children being brought before the juvenile courts, but the outcome of police action led to more punitive action being taken by the courts. Thus, the positive effects of the 1969 Act were effectively lost to black children and did not promote their specific interests. While one part of the legislation (under sections 2 and 15) offered children community resources as preventive measures, running counter to this was the over-use of the more punitive sections of the legislation for black children.

The mid-1960s were also significant for black children because this was the beginning of the period when transracial adoption was becoming accepted practice. Transracial adoption – placing black children with white families – was first introduced in response to the needs of childless white couples and the unavailability of white babies for adoption. It also came in response to the growing numbers of black children living in institutions and was based on the notion that black substitute families were unavailable. Views about the acceptability of transracial adoption were based on the thinking that all children were the same, and therefore the needs of black children were not perceived as different from those of white children. According to Small[11] this practice 'gained momentum with the philosophy of the assimilation of the immigrant child into society'.

The ideology surrounding the placement of black children emphasised that there were significant difficulties in finding substitute families for them. This encouraged the placement of black children in residential establishments. In their pursuit to find families for black children, a research project by ABAFA[12] further endorsed transracial placements. At this time the idea of the "melting pot" and the "colour-blind" approach became incorporated into social work practice and the placement of black children in white families became common practice. To quote from BAAF's Practice Note[13]: 'To be white or black did not matter. Colour was unimportant; we were all the same underneath.'

1970–1980

Two important pieces of legislation were passed in the mid 1970s: the Children Act 1975 and the Adoption Act 1976. Both had great significance for children needing long-term care and were built on the principle that the welfare of the child was to be the first and paramount consideration; the child was thus firmly established as the primary focus. The substantial provisions included changes in adoption laws and introduction of custodianship, and amendments to previous Children Acts.

The significance for black children

It is important to restate that black children had limited or, in some cases, no access to specific types of provision such as adoption and foster care. This was clearly highlighted in an important study conducted by Rowe and Lambert[14] which showed that one in every four children in their sample was black and was waiting in a residential establishment for substitute parents. Colour was identified as a barrier to successful placement and effectively kept black children in residential accommodation for all their childhood. A similar study by Raynor[15] also found a disproportionate number of black children living in residential institutions. Small[16] argued that while black children were trapped in the welfare system, policies and practices were developing that prevented the development of same-race placements. The then DHSS had stated in its practice guide[17] that the ability to retain identity was an important part of a child's life. The guidance did not, however, reinforce the need for same-race placements, but rather the need for environments where a dual culture was acknowledged, highlighting only the problems of language. The report recommended more training for foster carers.

Growing concern within the black community about the experiences of black children in care led to the Soul Kids Campaign. Its purpose was to launch a recruitment campaign targeted at the Caribbean community to highlight the need for foster and adoptive parents for black children in care. It also sought to sensitise and educate white professionals to the advantages of placing black children with families who reflected their own racial and cultural group. Even though the results were not spectacular, some observations were apparent: the first was the acute lack of social work resources for black children and the second, the prevailing attitudes of professionals who questioned the need for black substitute parents for black children.

There was also mounting concern amongst black professionals and the wider black community about the widespread practice and deleterious effects of transracial placements.[18,19,20] This led to the setting up of the Association of Black Social Workers and Allied Professionals (ABSWAP). They argued that while there was no doubt that white carers could meet a black child's needs for essentials and other material necessities, they strongly questioned their ability 'to equip the black child with the necessary psychological tools to develop appropriate identity and deal appropriately with an oppressive racist society'.[21]

1980s – the present

The Child Care Act 1980

Concerns that many black children were taken into voluntary care and never returned to their families were voiced in the Evidence to the House of Commons Social Services Committee in 1983.[22] The Committee drew attention to a London borough's statistics showing that while only one-third of white children were received in care under section 2, as many as two-thirds of black children were received into care. Concerns were voiced by Pennie and Best[23] that many black parents allowed their children to be received into voluntary care as a temporary measure . . . yet they were never returned to them.

Although the emphasis since 1948 was that parents should resume care of their children as soon as was practicable, the local authority could, under section 2(1)(c), determine whether the child should be removed from parents into care, or detained in care under section 2(2), or discharged from care under section 2(3). The Department of Health's statistics for the year ending 1990[24] showed that 38 per cent or 22,435 of the children in care were in voluntary care under section 2. However, figures for black children were not available as these were not recorded.

Private fostering

The Foster Care Act 1980 provided for children in private foster care. However, non-specific provisions meant that local authorities could make their own interpretations of the legislation. The main feature was that the local authority had responsibility to supervise such placements. However, children who were privately fostered remained largely unprotected, despite unsatisfactory conditions in the homes in which they were boarded out. Safeguards for privately fostered children compared poorly with those in local authority foster homes. Ellis[25] made the point that while the Boarding Out Regulations 1948 and the Children Acts of 1948 and 1975 all demanded that material standards and suitability of foster parents were satisfactory, appropriate safeguards were not put in place with regard to privately fostered children.

One of the only research studies on private fostering was conducted by Holman in the 1960s.[26] This study exposed lower standards of supervision for these children (most of whom were born of West African parents) in comparison with children accommodated by the local authority; a high proportion of these children remained in unsuitable placements with limited intervention, even in cases where social workers recognised the placements as unsuitable.

As recently as 1993 the African Family Advisory Service estimated that 6,000 to 9,000 West African children, mostly from Nigeria, were privately fostered in Britain. Of concern were the lack of care standards, inadequate medical care, educational under-achievement and behavioural difficulties; the most damaging consequences were the level and nature of disruption children experienced.

Privately fostered children leave care at the much earlier age of 16 compared to children placed with local authority foster carers, and have no entitlement to after care services unless they are disabled, in which case they remain privately fostered until the age of 18. In this sense they are like all other young people who come under the category of being "in need" of assistance and advice.

The Children Act 1989

The Children Act 1989 came as a result of the need for reforms in child care legislation. A report by the House of Commons Social Services Select Committee was followed by a consultation period in 1984–85. Nine research studies looking into the circumstances of children in 49 local authorities (over 2,000 children) were published by the Department of Health as the well known *Decisions in Child Care*[27] and were also influential in shaping what would become the 1989 Act. Barn[28] observed that 'not one of these nine studies focused on the race dimension'. Change also came in the wake of inquiries[29,30,31] into some of the most tragic cases of child deaths, among them, Jasmine Beckford, Tyra Henry and Kimberley Carlile.

The social consequences for black children coming into care from the 1960s onwards included being disadvantaged by racism as manifested in the views, attitudes and behaviours of white professionals and white carers. Coombe[32] described this era as a time when black children were received into care with "religious zeal". ABSWAP[33] argued that the implications for black children were that existing child care policy was destroying the black family as a unit by its disregard of the specific problems posed by transracial placements and through the lack of "ethnically sensitive" services.

The Children Act 1989 reinforced some general principles, the first of which is that the child's welfare is paramount (section 1(1)). Its uniqueness, however, was that for the first time in legislative history it recognised that Britain is a multiracial and multicultural society. This recognition led to section 22(5)(a) which stipulates that: '. . . a local authority shall give due consideration to the child's religious persuasion, racial origin and cultural and linguistic background.'

The Act charged local authorities 'not to allow or cause the child to be brought up in any religious persuasion other than that in which he would have been brought up if no Order had been made'.

The significance for black children

The needs of black children were described in the report submitted in the early 1980s to the Social Services Committee[34] as including:
- the need for a positive black identity;
- teaching of techniques for survival skills in a racist society;
- the development of cultural and linguistic skills; and
- a balanced bicultural experience to encourage healthy integration of personality.

The Children Act 1989 required local authorities to give issues of race and culture 'due consideration' in all services delivered by the local authority for children defined to be "in need": services such as fostering, residential care and day care services are included. The Act also introduced new regulations for private fostering in recognition of the need for better protection for children in private arrangements, many of whom are black. Ahmad[35] noted that the Act underscored the welfare principle and therefore *all* sections apply to black children.

The National Children's Bureau[36] commented that the Act did not deal directly with race and culture in the placement of children. Morgan and Taylor[37] stated that the success or failure of the Act, as far as black children are concerned, would rest with the local authority's willingness to utilise resources in and for the black community.

MacDonald et al[38] made it clear that it was important to understand that the Act has application for *all* children regardless of colour, class, culture, gender, disability or ethnicity. However, MacDonald made two important points:
1. that the history and experience of black children and their families had been one of exclusion from welfare services which had 'subjected them to greater social control than their white counterparts'; and
2. that if the Children Act 1989 was to achieve its desired objective, then social work practitioners must address the issues of "race", culture, language and religion without which it would be impossible to meet the child's needs.

Preparation for leaving care and after care

The Children Act 1989 also recognised that young people leaving care are entitled to preparation prior to leaving care and after care support services whether they return to their families or not and regardless of whether they are looked after in local authority accommodation or in private or voluntary settings. The DoH Guidance and Regulations[39] state that under sections 24(1), 61(1) and 64(1) local authorities and voluntary agencies have a duty to prepare young people for leaving care or accommodation and must ensure that: 'Preparation for leaving care starts well before a young person ceases to be looked after or accommodated and is likely to continue well after he has done so.' Preparation must include three aspects:

- enabling young people to build and maintain relationships with others both general and sexual;
- enabling young people to develop self-esteem; and
- teaching practical and financial skills and knowledge.

Equally, the Children Act 1989 recognised that after care support was necessary and made provision for it by recommending that local authorities and voluntary agencies should continue to provide the following:

- advice and information;
- continued interest in the welfare of young people;
- assistance in cash or kind;
- facilitating a return to care if necessary; and
- support in education, training and accommodation.

Types of accommodation

Foster care

Foster homes were always viewed as a more positive alternative to residential care. Pringle and Naidoo[40] noted that both in law and practice, assumptions were made about blood ties and natural parenthood, yet there was very little support developed in the black community to ensure that parents could receive help in time of trouble. ABSWAP[41] argued that the 1980 Foster Care Act underscored middle-class values that were at variance with black family life and that the power vested in foster carers effectively alienated black children from their roots.

The needs of the child for warmth, love, security, discipline and a sense of identity are all regarded as crucial to psychological development. Not all children were considered suitable for foster care: children with disabilities, emotional difficulties, children committing offences and "coloured and mixed race" children found themselves excluded from what was deemed to be the better form of care. Black and mixed heritage children were placed in the same category as "handicapped" children and labelled "hard to place", a term very much in use during the 1970s and 80s. As such, their needs were not of paramount consideration as provided for by legislation, but were, in fact, substantially neglected.

Residential care

Residential care has always been regarded as the least attractive option for children but has been widely used by local authorities. Concerns about the effects of prolonged institutionalisation on patterns of behaviour have been frequently voiced. Despite the numbers of children placed in residential care, there has been a noticeable lack of research, as Rowe et al[42] stated, into the effects of different types of care different types of children. Studies by Berridge[43] published in 1985 and the

Social Services Inspectorate[44] on Children's Homes produced significant data with regards to regimes and standards. However, this research did not examine outcomes or make comparisons between homes or between residential care and foster care.

Black young people in residential care

In a study of children in long-term care, Pinder and Shaw[45] found that black children were more likely to be taken into care as a result of police referral on the grounds of delinquency, more likely to be in residential accommodation than in foster placements, and as having 'less useful relationships with social workers'. Similar findings by Triseliotis[46] pointed to lesser access to health services for black parents and a general tendency to pathologise the black family unit as unstable. Children themselves have spoken out about the negative and stigmatising effects of residential care. Research by Whittaker and Cox[47] showed that nearly half their sample of children had negative views of children's homes, and of these, half showed evidence of feeling stigmatised or labelled as a result of living in a children's home.

The research evaluating the impact of residential care on black children – on their "race", culture and identity – has been limited. Research completed during the 1970s, 1980s, and 1990s and critical reports making an impact on policy all failed to recognise the particular experiences of black children in residential care on the basis of their heritage and identity needs.

Access to education for young black people in care

The educational needs of black children, in particular those in local authority care, have raised concerns since 1967 when Fitzherbert[48] conducted one of the first descriptive studies of black children in care and found that a high percentage of children using child care services were black. Batta and Mawby[49] noted that although there was high usage of child care services by these minority groups, they had not been the subject of much attention. This was echoed in studies conducted by the CRE,[50] Jackson and Jackson[51] and Cheetham.[52]

In general, the research on children in care suggests that many black children who came into care were part of the overall debate about underachievement and substandard care. Since 1979, when the Rampton Report[53] addressed the causes for underachievement of West Indian children, there have been concerns about why black children leave school at an educational disadvantage. This underachievement was attributed to factors such as poor socio-economic conditions and institutional racism within the education system. A survey by the CRE[54] entitled *Learning in Terror* discovered that many black children were subjected to high levels of racial abuse and violent attacks within the school environment, at bus stops and on the streets. This was further substantiated by the Department for Education and Science[55] (DES) in 1985 and by Kelly and Cohen.[56] Concerns about exclusion from school have increased in recent years and have been taken up by the National Children's Bureau (NCB)[57] particularly in relation to children in the care system; they have pointed to ethnicity as one of the factors that encourages exclusion. National and regional studies have shown that black children and those from other minority ethnic groups have been disproportionately excluded.

In addressing the educational underachievement of black children in the care system, the NCB argued that these could not be separated from the following:

- Poor decisions in relation to placement;
- Unstable environments and lack of long-term planning which contribute to children and young people drifting into care; and
- Low priority given to educational needs by social services and education authorities.

IMMIGRATION LEGISLATION

The growth of the black population in Britain following the post-war era and particularly during the 1950s and 60s led to mounting concerns that immigration had to be controlled. As a result, controls were introduced under the Commonwealth Immigrants Act 1962 and were followed by severe curtailment of numbers in 1965 under the White Paper, *Immigration from the Commonwealth*.

The Commonwealth Immigrants Act 1968 was introduced following a powerful lobby against the rights of immigrants who had retained United Kingdom citizenship after independence of their countries of origin post-British colonialism. The exercise of rights to settle in Britain following economic and political difficulties in their own countries was met with hostility and this led to the government severely curtailing entry of immigrants from Asia and East Africa. By 1971 there was a rationalisation of immigration policy by controls and a distinction between immigrants on the grounds of "patriality", that is to say, descent. The British Nationality Act 1981 introduced three separate categories of citizenship. The most important factor relating to children was that they no longer acquired citizenship by birth in the United Kingdom but relied on descent and/or residence.

RACE RELATIONS LEGISLATION

The Race Relations Act 1976 placed a duty on local authorities to eliminate racial discrimination. In particular, section 71 imposed a duty on them to ensure that their functions were carried out with due regard to need, in an attempt to 'eliminate unlawful discrimination', and 'promote equal opportunity between persons of different racial groups' (section 71 (a)(b)).

The CRE Working Report[58] suggested that the Race Relations Act created an opportunity for social services departments to 'allow special provision to be made to meet certain needs of particular ethnic groups and permit certain kinds of positive action'. In 1977, the CRE reported that black children were significantly over-represented amongst the disadvantaged and that their special needs arose from their 'minority racial and cultural status'. It was argued that local authorities made limited use of the Race Relations Act 1976 to integrate its provisions into service delivery for black children in care and ensure anti-racist and anti-discriminatory practice.

MacDonald[59] noted that 15 years after the Race Relations Act was enforced, outlawing discriminatory practices, there has been limited evidence to show that the social work profession is using this legislation to 'rid itself of its oppressive force'. She argued that local authorities have not used this Act to forge a link between the quality and equity of social work practice and service delivery to black children and their families.

References

1 Home Office Circular, (1948a), 160, HMS0.

2 Bowlby J, *Attachment*, Hogarth Press, 1969.

3 Hurst Report of the Departmental Committee, *The Adoption of Children*, HMSO, 1954.

4 Williams F, *Social Policy: A critical introduction*, Polity Press, 1989.

5 Beveridge W, *Social Insurance and Allied Services, Cmd 6404*, HMSO, 1948.

6 Ingleby Report of the Committee, *Children and Young Persons, Cmnd 1191*, HMSO, 1960.

7 Pringle M and Naidoo S, *Early Childcare in Britain*, Gordon and Breach, 1975.

8 Seebohm Report of the Committee, *Local Authorities and Allied Personal Social Services*, HMSO, 1968.

9 Lambert J, *Crime, Police and Race Relations*, Oxford University Press, 1970.

10 Pearce K, *West Indian Boys in Community Home Schools*, Unpublished Thesis of the Diploma in Education, University of London, Institute of Education, published in abridged form in *Community Schools Gazette* 68, 6.7.8., 1974.

11 Small J, "Transracial placements: conflicts and contradictions", in Ahmed S, Cheetham J and Small J (eds), *Social Work with Black Children and their Families*, BAAF/Batsford, 1986. Reprinted 1990.

12 Association of British Adoption and Fostering Agencies, The Soul Kids Campaign, 1976.

13 British Agencies for Adoption & Fostering, *The Placement Needs of Black Children*, Practice Note 13, BAAF, 1987.

14 Rowe J and Lambert L, *Children Who Wait*, ABAFA, 1973.

15 Raynor L, *Adoption of Non-White Children in Britain*, Allen and Unwin, 1970.

16 See 11 above.

17 Department of Health, *Code of Practice: Access to children in care*, HMSO, 1984.

18 Small J, "The crisis in adoption", in *International Journal of Psychiatry*, 129–142, Spring 1984.

19 Divine D, "No Problems", *Caribbean Times*, 4 March 1983.

20 Chimezie A, "Transracial adoption of black children", *Social Work* 20, 296–301, 1975.

21 Association of Black Social Workers and Allied Professionals, *Black Children in Care*, Evidence to the House of Commons Social Services Committee, 1983.

22 Commission for Racial Equality, Working Party Report, *Submission to the House of Commons Social Services Select Committee Inquiry into Children in Care*, CRE, 1978.

23 Pennie P and Best F, *How the Black Family is Pathologised by the Social Services System*, ABSWAP, 1990.

24 Department of Health Statistics Year Ending 1990, HMSO.

25 Ellis J (ed), *West African Families in Britain: A meeting of two cultures*, Routledge and Kegan Paul, 1978.

26 Holman R, *Trading in Children*, Routledge and Kegan Paul, 1968.

27 Department of Health and Social Security, *Social Work Decisions in Child Care: Recent research findings and their implications*, HMSO, 1985.

28 Barn R, *Black Children in the Public Care System*, BAAF/Batsford, 1993.

29 Beckford J, *A Child in Trust*, The Report of the Panel of Inquiry into the circumstances surrounding the death of Jasmine Beckford, London Borough of Brent, 1985.

30 *Whose Child – A Report of the Public Inquiry into the Death of Tyra Henry*, London Borough of Lambeth, 1987.

31 *A Child in Mind – The Report of the Commission of Inquiry into the Circum-stances Surrounding the Death of Kimberley Carlile*, London Borough of Greenwich, 1987.

32 Coombe V and Little A (eds), *Race and Social Work*, Routledge, 1986.

33 See 21 above.

34 See 21 above.

35 Ahmad B, "Child care and ethnic minorities", in Kahan B (ed), *Child Care Research Policy and Practice*, Hodder and Stoughton, 1989.

36 National Children's Bureau, *Working with the Children Act 1989: An introduction for practitioners in education, health and and social work*, NCB, 1991.

37 Morgan C and Taylor A, *A Study of Black Young People Leaving Care*, Social Services Research, Nos 5/6, 10–24, 1987.

38 MacDonald S, *All Equal Under the Act?*, Race Equality Unit, 1992.

39 Department of Health, *The Children Act: Guidance and regulations*, Vol 3, HMSO, 1991.

40 See 18 above.

41 See 21 above.

42 Rowe J, Hundleby M and Garnett L, *Child Care Now: A survey of placement patterns*, BAAF, 1989.

43 Berridge D, *Children's Homes*, Blackwell, 1985.

44 Department of Health and Social Security, *Social Work Inspection of Community Homes*, 1985.

45 Pinder R and Shaw M, *Coloured Children in Long Term Care*, Unpublished Report, Leicester University, School of Social Work, 1974.

46 Triseliotis J P (ed), *Social Work with Immigrant Clients*, Oxford University Press, 1972.

47 Whittaker D and Cox J, *The Experience of Residential Care from the Perspective of Children, Parents and Care-Givers*, Children in Care, University of York, 1992.

48 Fitzherbert K, *West Indian Children in London*, Bells and Sons, 1967.

49 Batta I and Mawby R, "Children in local authority care: a monitoring of racial differences in Bradford", *Policy and Politics* 9:2, 1981.

50 See 22 above.

51 Jackson B and Jackson S, *Childminder*, Routledge and Kegan Paul, 1979.

52 Cheetham J, *Social Services for Ethnic Minorities in Britain and the USA*, Research Thesis, 1981.

53 *Rampton Report of the Committee of Inquiry into the Education of Children from Ethnic Minority Groups: West Indian children in our schools*, HMSO, 1981.

54 Commission for Racial Equality, *Learning in Terror*, CRE, 1988.

55 Department of Education and Science, *Education for All: The Swan Report*, HMSO, 1985.

56 Kelly E and Cohen T, *Racism in Schools: New research evidence*, Trentham Books, 1988.

57 National Children's Bureau, *Exclusion from School*, Highlight no 136, NCB and Barnardo's, 1995.

58 See 22 above.

59 See 38 above.

2 Themes in the literature on leaving care

This chapter presents a brief overview of the literature that exists on children and young people leaving care. It is estimated that approximately 10,000 16 to 17-year-olds leave care to live independently each year. According to the Department of Health (DoH) records,[1] in 1985 over 7,700 young people aged 18 left care in England and Wales. The National Children's Bureau[2] published statistics which showed that at the end of March 1990, 6,239 young people were legally discharged from care on reaching the age of 18. In 1991, the DoH recorded that 5,100 young people were legally discharged from care; of these, 53 per cent moved to independence from residential care and 30 per cent moved to independence from foster care.

The past two decades have revealed a general lack of knowledge about what happens to young people after they leave care, and how well prepared or not they are to do so. The themes in the literature on the subject have shown the following:
- poor accommodation and high representation in homelessness statistics
- poverty and high unemployment;
- lack of educational achievement;
- high representation in the criminal justice system;
- lack of financial support after leaving care;
- isolation and loneliness; and
- poor and unco-ordinated response from local authorities.

The plight of young people leaving care had not been given any attention in terms of research until the mid to late 1970s when some descriptive studies were published. The Barnardo's study, *Leaving Care*, conducted by Godek,[3] *After Care Who Cares?* by Mulvey[4] and *Growing Up in Care* by Kahan[5] were among the first studies to consider the experiences of young people leaving care. These early studies led to an understanding about the vulnerability of young people leaving residential institutions and substitute families. They also highlighted some revealing information: young people leaving care were not a homogeneous group, and their pre-care and in-care experiences differed depending on background, culture and ethnicity; a high percentage of young people experienced disruption in their placements and experienced multiple moves, instability and an inconsistent care pattern throughout their stay in care; and links with family and community often tended to be severed, particularly for those spending longer periods in care. This frequently resulted in stress associated with feelings of rejection and loss and a distinct lack of knowledge about their heritage – this was particularly true for young black people who were brought up in predominantly white settings. Of central importance was the disturbing finding that young people received little or no preparation for leaving care and independent living after care.

The second wave of research, in the 1980s, and which made an invaluable contribution to the knowledge base and policy development was that of Stein and Carey[6] who brought to light the harrowing experiences of young people leaving the care system. In 1984 a Parliamentary Committee considered that local authorities had a general statutory obligation both to prepare those in care for leaving and to provide after care services. Alongside this were messages delivered by young people themselves. In the 1980s, the campaigning work of the National Association for Young People in Care (NAYPIC) became widely associated with the views of young people in care and leaving care, and First Key, a national voluntary organisation for advising young people was also set up. Equally important was the setting up of the voluntary organisation, Who Cares? Trust. All these organisations sought to and succeeded in making known the views of young people about their own in-care experiences, thereby contributing significantly to raising awareness amongst professionals charged with the responsibility of looking after them. The third significant development was the debate regarding the status given to leaving care and preparation for young people. Research studies conducted in the mid to late 1980s by Fisher et al,[7] the DoH[8] and Berridge and Cleaver[9] were all important landmarks and informed the Children Act 1989, giving young people a higher profile and promoting good practice in terms of the duties and responsibilities of the local authority.

A variety of projects and leaving care schemes also played an important role. An investigative study by Biehal et al[10] in evaluating different leaving care schemes in three local authorities provided valuable insights showing different interventions and their outcomes.

Homelessness

Homelessness is a major problem facing young people who leave care: accounts from young people in research conducted by Stein and Carey[11] showed that accommodation was often unsatisfactory and that young people moved frequently. This was reinforced by Biehal et al[12] who noted that there was a high degree of mobility in the early months after leaving care and that leaving care schemes eased possible crisis situations by finding accommodation at short notice, in many cases in a few weeks or days.

Organisations concerned with homelessness have also frequently emphasised the links between leaving care and being homeless. Centrepoint, an organisation providing accommodation for homeless young people, disclosed in their Annual Report in 1991[13] that two out of five young people on the streets had lived in children's homes or with foster carers. During a six-month period in 1993, 29 per cent of all young people seen by Centrepoint had been in care and almost half were between the ages of 16 and 17.

Education and unemployment

Research has consistently demonstrated that restricted educational opportunities for young people in the care system have affected adversely their chances of higher education and finding employment. A survey conducted by Leeds University[14] found that out of a sample of 183, only one person had an A level and 22 or 15 per cent of the sample had GCSEs at grades A–C. This was abysmal when compared to the general population. It was estimated in 1994 by the Audit Commission[15] that up to 40 per cent of young people living in children's homes were non-school attenders and, moreover, that this alarming state of affairs had not been identified and addressed as a serious problem facing young people in the care system.

Poverty and financial stability

Financial stability is crucial to a young person's ability to become independent. However, poverty and high unemployment have been consistent themes in the literature. Burgess[16] placed young care leavers on the lowest tier of the labour market, showing that they tended to occupy the lowest paid positions in semi-skilled and unskilled work. Mulvey[17] observed that young people discharged from care were not necessarily more disadvantaged than any other young person who leaves home, but that leaving care represented one disadvantage among many.

Local authority responses

A study commissioned by the London Borough Regional Planning Committee into local authority policy and practice on leaving care, conducted by Bonnerjea,[18] found that local authorities were not fulfilling their responsibilities to young people leaving care. Bonnerjea noted that young care leavers were particularly vulnerable because of external factors such as the rise in unemployment, cutbacks in social security provision and a decline in cheap housing. Broad[19] also argued that young people in care were among the most vulnerable people in the country. He declared the findings of an After Care Consortium survey which canvassed the views of staff working with 1,538 young people in 25 projects in 25 different areas. The survey found an increased demand for services – believed to be due to increased homelessness and a high dependence on support from the state.

The After Care Consortium report by the National Children's Bureau found that only 76 per cent of local authorities (21) had policies and procedures on leaving care. Of the 21 local authorities with some provision, one local authority stated that procedures were in place and were always followed; 13 local authorities stated that procedures were mostly followed; six local authorities said that procedures were sometimes followed; and one local authority stated that procedures were hardly ever followed. Eight per cent of authorities had no policy or procedures and 16 per cent did not respond.

In *Social Work Today* a campaign on behalf of care leavers was reported over several weeks by Rickford,[20] Morris,[21] Dibbin,[22] Kahan[23] and Saddington.[24] Without fail, all reported a lack of resources for young people leaving care and a failure of local authorities to make adequate provision for them. Kahan's article went a step further in highlighting the poor educational achievements of children in care and asked to what extent they were bound to fail.

An important study published in 1992 by Garnett[25] involved interviews with 183 care leavers and 135 social workers from six local authorities. Garnett emphasised the importance of relating policy to practice and challenged local authorities to begin by 'examining how well they are currently meeting young people's needs'.

Black young people leaving care

The literature review could not establish that there was a significant amount of research or serious study conducted in the UK into the specific issues facing young black people leaving care. The study most consistently pointed to as providing some evidence is the First Key study,[26] funded and produced by the Commission for Racial Equality (CRE). Based on information derived from three London boroughs and a number of preparation for independence units, data were gathered regarding the circumstances of young black people with experience of the care system. It reported disparity between the three boroughs in the way they made or did not make adequate provision for young black people leaving care. A study by Biehal[27] which included 25 young people of black and mixed heritage background in their sample of 183 found that black children of mixed heritage were proportionally the highest group being "looked after". A significant and important finding was that black children were two and a half times more likely than white children to come into care earlier and remain in care longer. However, very little was said about the impact of this finding on leaving care and after care outcomes. Notwithstanding these new findings, there remains a gap in knowledge about the extent to which black young people are prepared for leaving care and subsequent difficulties they may face after leaving care.

Black and In Care, an organisation formed to raise the profile of and give a voice to black young people in care, held a series of workshops in 1984. The conference concluded that:
- residential units were staffed mainly by white people;
- there were insignificant numbers of black staff in management positions;
- there was overt and covert racism within the care system;
- the effects of the loss of racial identity were very strong and remained with the young black people long after care had ended.

In the conference report and video, *Black and In Care*,[28] young black people spoke about the magnitude of the problem. The lack of preparation offered meant that they were effectively incapable of making links with the black community. Many saw themselves as white. The policy of a "colour-blind" approach was felt to be unhelpful and lacked a black perspective in social work.

The Commission for Racial Equality issued a statement of purpose in 1992 which was aimed at raising standards of work with young people. They recommended improved consultation with young people and a detailed focus on organisational policies in terms of monitoring, reviewing and evaluating policies.

Consequences for young black people

In 1992, Centrepoint's publication, *A National Scandal*,[30] reported on youth homelessness and claimed that young black people were at a greater disadvantage than their white peers and suffered from 'direct and indirect discrimination'. According to the report this was 'demonstrated throughout the UK by landlords who will not let to young black people, and by bureaucratic systems which shut them out. Young black people also face discrimination in employment and on Youth Training Schemes, which has a knock-on effect on their access to housing.'

Morgan and Taylor[31] observed that an additional problem for black care leavers was their lack of a strong racial identity which could lead to isolation and loneliness, coupled with a lack of information about organisations that are likely to offer help. A further problem cited by Pennie[32] was that black young people leaving care were more likely to have experienced contact with the juvenile justice system, which could substantially diminish their chances of gaining employment. This accords with the views of Centrepoint which stressed that young people leaving custody experienced severe problems in finding employment and accommodation. In terms of preparation for leaving care, Carton[33] evaluated a programme set up to prepare adolescents for life after foster care. She stated that: 'Black foster parents can be a valuable source of such knowledge to agencies, and they are in a key position to advocate for services needed by youths approaching discharge from care.'

The above view was supported by research conducted by the National Foster Care Association (NFCA). Their survey, reported in *After Care – Making the most of foster care* by Fry,[34] found that young black people were more likely to be homeless in proportion to their percentage in the population. This research cited direct and indirect racism within the public sector as a major cause of discrimination in the housing sector. With reference to the report, *Young, Black and Homeless in London*,[35] Fry adhered to the view that financial and other supports, including training opportunities, be given to black foster carers to enable them to 'support vulnerable young people as they leave care and afterwards'.

References

1 Department of Health and Social Security, *Children in Care in England and Wales*, March, 1985.

2 National Children's Bureau, *Working with the Children Act 1989: An introduction for practitioners in education, health and social work*, NCB, 1991.

3 Godek S, *Leaving Care: A case study approach to the difficulties children face in leaving residential care*, Barnardo's, 1976.

4 Mulvey T, *After Care Who Cares: A study of young people who have left care at the statutory leaving age of 18*, University of Essex, 1977.

5 Kahan B, *Growing up in Care*, Blackwell, 1979.

6 Stein M and Carey K, *Leaving Care*, Blackwell, 1986.

7 Fisher M, Marsh P, Phillips D and Sainsbury E, *In and Out of Care*, Batsford, 1989.

8 Department of Health, *Social Work Decisions in Child Care*, HMSO, 1985.

9 Berridge D and Cleaver H, *Foster Home Breakdown*, Blackwell, 1987.

10 Biehal N, Clayden J, Stein M and Wade J, *Moving on: Young people and leaving care schemes*, HMSO, 1995.

11 See 6 above.

12 See 10 above.

13 Centrepoint, *Helping Young People*, Annual Report, 1990–1991.

14 University of Leeds, "Prepared for living", in Stein M and Frost N, *Working with Young People Leaving Care*, HMSO, 1995.

15 Audit Commission, *Seen but Not Heard*, HMSO, 1994.

16 Burgess C, *In Care and into Work*, Tavistock, 1981.

17 See 4 above.

18 Bonnerjea L, *Leaving Care in London*, London Borough Regional Planning Committee, 1990.

19 Broad B, *Improving Practice and Policy in After Care Work*, a report on the National Children's Bureau Aftercare Consortium Conference, Henson A (ed), First Key, 1994.

20 Rickford F, "Moving on", *Social Work Today* 24:5, 16–17, 1992.

21 Morris P, "Too much too young", *Social Work Today* 24:7, 18–19, 1992.

22 Dibbin J, "Parting time", *Social Work Today* 24:8, 16–17, 1992.

23 Kahan B, "Born to fail?", *Social Work Today* 24:11, 16–19, 1992.

24 Saddington A, "Big ideas", *Social Work Today* 24:6, 16–18, 1992.

25 Garnett L, *Leaving Care and After*, National Children's Bureau, 1992.

26 First Key, *A Study of Young Black People Leaving Care*, CRE, 1987.

27 See 10 above.

28 *Black and In Care Report, Conference and Video*, Report of a conference by the Black and In Care Steering Group, 1984.

29 Commission for Racial Equality, *Young and Equal: A standard for racial equality in services working with young people*, CRE, 1995.

30 Centrepoint, *A National Scandal: Survey of published information on young people leaving care*, Centrepoint, 1990.

31 Morgan C and Taylor A, *A Study of Young Black People Leaving Home*, Social Sciences Research 5–6, 10–12, 1987.

32 Pennie P, "Black children need the richness of black family life", *Social Work Today*, 2 February 1987.

33 Carton A, *Building on the Strengths of Black Foster Families*, Child Welfare League of America, 1990, USA.

34 Fry E, *After Care – Making the most of foster care*, National Foster Care Association, 1992.

35 *Young, Black and Homeless in London*, Report by Ujimaa Housing Association and Barnardo's in Fry E, *After Care: Making the most of foster care*, National Foster Care Association, 1992.

"Race", culture and identity

This chapter offers an introduction to the concepts of "race", culture and identity and signifies their importance for black people with special reference to children and young black people separated from their birth families.

The term "race" has many meanings and has historically been used to denote or categorise people into specific groups. In general the term is often used interchangeably with colour, heredity and nationality. For the purposes of this study I offer the definition used by Barker and Moran[1] who describe "race" as:

> . . . a social concept by which groups and individuals differentiate other groups from themselves. Physical appearance and cultural indicators are the key criteria of such labelling processes.

The social concept of "race" emphasises that physical appearance and culture are key signs for labelling. Husbands[2] argued that the concept cannot be reduced to simplistic explanations because it denotes a 'highly complex body of emotive ideas'; thus, colonialism, capitalism, biological categorisations and political factors have all been part of the "race" debate. Colour is one of the significant factors in the process of categorisation because it makes distinctions and is a sign of group membership, as are characteristics based on physical and cultural differences. "Race" has also been used to determine levels of ability in terms of superiority and inferiority; skin colour has been cited as a prime factor in determining difference. Thus, the concept of "race" has been embedded within a theoretical framework that seeks to reinforce value-laden notions of difference and categorisation. For the purposes of this study, the importance of "race" focuses on the manifestations of labelling for people with black skins who live in a predominantly white society and who are adversely affected by the outcome of racism. Baker and Moran[3] stated that for black citizens, the skin colour will always place them in a different category to other minority ethnic groups who are white.

Ethnicity is a term commonly used to acknowledge the difference between groups and is often used in preference to the word "race", which is placed in quotes to show that the term is not being used to make false biologically determined classifications, as has frequently been the case, but in a way that classifies people by placing them in specific groups which carry with them cultural characteristics.

Racism

Racism has been defined by Lorde as 'the belief in the inherent superiority of one race over all others and thereby the right to dominance, manifest and implied'.[4] Thus it is a value system that is negative and based on stereotypes. Thompson[5] contended that negative stereotypes serve to pathologise individuals, families and cultures that deviate from the dominant white norm.

Penderhughes[6] provided a useful synopsis of the consequences of racism:
- It creates a state of psychological stress.
- It forces people to behave in destructive ways, to project and transfer blame to justify their own reality.
- It creates confusion about the meaning of being white.

- It creates a delusion of superiority, with an inability to experience the true self, due to arrogance and disdain it embodies for those who are non-white.
- It threatens a sense of positive self-worth.
- It prevents white people from experiencing and accepting humanity because there is an inability to empathise with people of colour.

Individual racism is that which is manifested as a result of a person's value systems and beliefs, and can permeate an individual's attitudes, behaviours and perceptions, including in the workplace.

Social workers, like any other professionals, bring their individual value systems to the social work interface and stereotypical ideas about people from minority ethnic groups undoubtedly affect practice. Negative values can influence the social worker's interaction with black children and assumptions about patterns of parenting and childcare may lead to perceptions of weakness rather than strength. Cheetham[7] said that individual racism can affect assessment and is 'a mainspring for social work, against the belief in the capacity for growth and change'.

Institutional racism is a broader concept and is defined as ranging from economic and other social systems which intentionally or unintentionally keep black people in subordinate positions to those rules and practices of individual and public bodies which unwittingly discriminate against people.

One of the most worrying factors in relation to the organisation of personal social services is the extent to which racism is imbued in institutional practices. Institutional racism occurs when 'practices have an adverse impact on blacks as a group'.[8] These adverse effects serve to perpetuate racism, manifesting themselves in poor services and poor outcomes for children in care. Dominelli[9] argued that institutional racism was a part of the normal and routine workings of social work policy and practice, and Hall[10] argued that the major problem confronting institutions such as the personal social services was the structural position of minority communities in Britain and their relationship to social work agencies. The problem rests primarily with "power relations" which allow themselves to be manifested in major areas of service provision such as housing, employment, policing, and in financial provision for community needs.

Significance of "race" for black children in care

Dominelli[11] argued that despite the fact that Britain is ethnically pluralistic, this has not been reflected in practice or service delivery. Since black children are subjected to the same categorisation as black adults, this has had the effect of emphasising differences and neglecting needs. Ahmad[12] pointed out that one of the fundamental issues for black children is how they become 'victims of ignorance, dilemma, unawareness, subjective judgement, insensitivity and prejudice on the part of the social worker'. The outcome, she argued, is that children pay the price for lack of awareness of the impact of "race" on social work intervention. Considering the effects of residential care on black children, Coombe[13] stated that there was a need for greater awareness of the effects of the racism which operates at individual and institutional levels within the care system.

One of the major errors has been to treat all children as if their needs were the same, commonly known as the "colour-blind" approach. This has led to a lack of understanding of the true needs of black children. It is important to understand that black children in care have needs that are specifically related to their "race".

Personal care needs in terms of hair and skin care are important aspects of their identity development as are dietary and religious needs. ABSWAP[14] also stated that black children in care must be offered 'survival skills for living in a racist society'.

A study by Fitzherbert[15] as long ago as 1967 made some interesting findings that related to racial discrimination and disadvantage experienced by black children in the care system. He contended that the underpinning of conventional social work, and in particular casework methods, were located within a white value system and frame of reference. The part that racism has to play in social work practice has also been explored by Ely and Denny[16], Dominelli[17], Ahmad[18], Cheetham[19] and Husbands[20]. They all refer to some of the dominant perspectives influencing the "race" debate including the tendency to present black people as either problematic or victims.

EMPOWERMENT THEORY AND SOCIAL WORK

The development of racial theories and the stigma attached to "race" have undoubtedly influenced social work. Penderhughes[21] argued that those who worked in the caring services were trapped in biases and structures because

> *The ideas, attitudes, feelings and perceptions . . . are held tenaciously.*
> *Many of them are hidden or obscure despite the fact that they heavily*
> *determine people's behaviour and cross-racial situations.*

One of the conceptual frameworks which has been applied in social work practice is that of Empowerment Theory. The work of Solomon[22] has helped to develop thinking on this approach as a task of social work practice that can increase the power base of the service user. Empowerment is particularly concerned with the experiences of black people because it recognises the damaging effects of powerlessness and negative valuations. Its specific purpose is to develop strategies that will redress the balance between professionals and service users, and thus strengthen the social worker's ability to work in non-derogatory and non-racist ways. To work in this way is to acknowledge the three levels of development to which Solomon has pointed:
- This model values positive experiences of the family in a way that enhances confidence and competence in social relations and interactions.
- It reinforces ability to negotiate social relationships and to understand how to relate to large-scale institutions such as school, social services departments, etc.
- It encourages acceptance and leads people to perform well in valued social roles.

As far as service provision to black families is concerned, empowerment theory will assist social workers to value the positive contributions that a black family can offer and lead to improved services for black children and families.

Ely and Denny[23] promote the black professional perspective, that of anti-racist practice. This perspective seeks to articulate logical principles and strategies that will bring about a significant change in response to black service users.

CULTURE

Culture as a concept is clearly important to this study. It is a major consideration of the way in which black children are reared and develop. Within the context of their own families, culture has specific meaning and is of fundamental importance to their existence. When one begins to consider the nature and importance of culture it is, according to Nobles,[24] the process by which

> . . . *symbolism, meanings, definitions, feelings, attitudes, values and behaviours are transmitted to each and every member of a group.*

Haviland[25] argued that culture is an important aspect of self-awareness and that it is the attachment of positive value to the self, but being able to identify self on its own is not enough; a process of learning is vital:

> *Perception precedes conception, which involves a cultural definition of self and in this definition language plays a crucial role.*

Chimezie[26] offered a useful review of the ways in which culture has been conceptualised. He pointed out that these have been divided into two distinct areas, affirmative and negative: theorists who support the affirmative line contend that there is a distinctive black culture, but with differences in the degree to which they can be traced to African heritage; the negative school of thought believes that there is no distinctive black culture, and thus attributes differences between black and white people to class differences, degrees of poverty and social pathology.

Significance for black children separated from their families

Developments in the knowledge base of the effects of separation and loss on young children have influenced decisions about the need for care outside the family network. For black children who are separated from their family and extended network of relationships, some of the most basic cultural needs are neglected. Ahmed[27] recommended the need for sensitivity in service provision and the need for carers to understand the pain that black children suffer through separation from their own culture: 'It is important for carers to establish how children really feel about breaking parental instruction and family taboos.'

For black children in care the debate is concerned with how cultural transmission is possible when measures have not been taken to sustain racial and cultural identity. This is a point made by Ely and Denny[28] when they said that all children in care have a need to sustain their cultural identity, but this is more profound for black children who are surrounded exclusively by white images. They argued that the wish of social workers to work with minority ethnic groups must be accompanied by a deeper understanding than 'the usual casework theory or general social work training'. It includes an understanding of 'shared group history of migration, and the struggle to sustain existence and identity'.

Cheetham[29] noted that black children in care did not have the tendency to become fluent in two cultures, but became children 'who have lost the capacity to identify, feel and communicate readily with members of their community of origin'.

The black perspective within social work puts forward a strong argument for "race" and culture to be guiding principles in the placement of children for adoption and fostering. While there is recognition by some local authorities that black substitute families are most likely to meet the needs of black children, there is still resistance to placing black children with black families. Black professionals have consistently argued that the practice of transracial placements stems from the pathologising of black families and is leading to cultural genocide.[30] This view is highlighted in an article by Wilson[31] in which she pointed to two issues. Firstly, culture is integral to identity and the maintenance of cultural links. Secondly, transracial placements can 'substantially affect the child's perception of culture and racism'. If the child's culture is to be validated, Penderhughes[32] suggested that service providers must understand the variations that exist within culture and its role in providing 'strength, connectedness and a sense of identity'.

The role of culture in preparation for leaving care

The *Review of Child Care Law*[33] stated that the foundations for leaving care resided with the

> . . . *quality of the young person's experience throughout his or her stay in care. There is a danger in believing that preparation for leaving care is some specially devised programme to be applied only when a young person is approaching the end of his or her stay in care.*

In order that black young people do not suffer cultural deficits, adequate preparation for leaving care requires detailed attention to the role of culture. In so doing the young person is enabled to develop what Maluccio et al[34] described as 'hard skills' and 'intangible or soft skills'. Cultural preparation is a tangible skill because it encourages self-esteem and is essential for negotiating and interacting with individuals and groups in the community. Promoting contact between young people and their families, as is stipulated in the Children Act 1989, will allow culture to be transmitted. There is a recognition, according to Frost and Stein,[35] that 'contact may be particularly significant for black young people whose needs may not be met if they are cared for in predominantly white settings'. The black perspective would argue categorically that contact *is* (not may be) extremely significant to the black child and young person.

RACIAL IDENTITY

> *By some accounts identity is defined as one component of an individual's overall self-concept. It involves the adoption of certain personal attitudes, feelings, characteristics and behaviours (personal identity) and the identification with a larger group of people who share those characteristics.*[36]

Like cultural identity, racial identity is crucial to this study, since it accounts for a number of important developmental stages in a process that results in self-esteem. There are several theoretical definitions of identity, but the problem with these definitions is that they do not reside within a black frame of reference. Barnes[37] drew attention to the fact that when well-established theoretical frameworks are applied to black children and youths, they have not emphasised the importance of the black community as a positive reference group in identity formation.

Considerable difficulties can arise for children who are separated from their own racial group, not only while in care but also long after leaving the care system. A number of studies have pointed to the detrimental effects of the care experience on the racial identity of black children who have been placed in isolated white environments. Tajfel[38] noted that identity also included 'that part of an individual's self-concept which derives from his knowledge of his membership of a social group (or groups) together with the emotional significance attached to that membership'. This is clearly an active and ongoing process.

A framework for understanding racial identity

The importance of racial identity for black children should be understood from the point of social work intervention with and responses to black children and families.

Tizard and Phoenix[39] emphasised the need to distinguish between identity and self-concept. They argued that there is an intrinsic difference between racial identity and self-concept and hypothesised that it is possible for a young black person to have negative feelings about racial identity and at the same time have a positive concept of themselves. For the purposes of this study the definition of racial identity offered by Banks[40] will suffice in so far as it relates to

> . . . how a child sees him or herself in relation to his or her racial group and their own goodness of fit within that group.

The background of research into racial identity dates back to 1936 when Harowitz[41] and two American psychologists found that black children rejected their own "racial" group and showed preference for white groups. The research of Clark and Clark[42] provided the model for subsequent studies conducted throughout the 1950s and well into the 1960s. The main concern of these early studies was the way black children did not show preference for people of the same colour. These studies concentrated on children between the ages of three to seven years. The well-known work of Goodman[43] and Milner[44] pointed to the way in which young children developed an awareness of self and of others in relation to racial identity. Milner highlighted the socialisation process as a strong contributory factor in the way that children acquire attitudes and identity. He noted such factors as direct and indirect tuition in which teaching and observation are involved. Milner's research was conducted in England. His comparative study concentrated on the negative self-image of Asian and West Indian children. He first established that West Indian culture had a British component to it which he called the 'white bias'. This bias was enhanced by the children's positive feelings towards white people and their aspirations to assimilate. However, the Asian children were more insulated because of their strong sense of identity and separate culture. This was also a strong theme in some of the American studies which showed that black children were internalising the racial values imposed on them by the dominant white group. Moreover, he found that they had difficulty in identifying with their own racial group. Milner concluded that

> . . . it seemed likely that this response towards racism would be more prevalent among West Indian children than among the Asian children.

Milner showed that while West Indian children were under considerable pressure to accept imposed white values, Asian children were far more resistant to it.

Erikson,[45] who has written extensively on identity, saw it as the creation of sameness, and stressed the importance of affinity of personal or individual identity and communal or group identity.

Identity and the adolescent years

The adolescent years are recognised as turbulent and perplexing. This is a time of intense questioning and seeking of answers that will help to make sense of the world. There is a vast body of theory that points to adolescence as a period of change, crisis, intense self-analysis and self-criticism. For many young people who have had an experience in care this is a crucial time in their development. Logan[46] stated that for black youth there was an added problem, the nature of which rests with identifying and making conscious attempts to reconcile self with a sense of one's people and evaluating standards that have been set according to 'white norms for self-measurement'.

The well-known studies of Gill and Jackson[47] examined a number of factors that determined racial identity. They found that black children who were brought up in a white-dominated context with very little contact with black people ultimately viewed themselves as effectively white. The work of Watson[48] suggested that many children born in Britain are caught between two cultures with the result that they are estranged from their parents' generation, but also do not fit into the dominant culture. This is a doubly difficult task for black youngsters who have not had the opportunity to be socialised within their own culture.

The role of the family and significant others

Identity development in relation to black children and young people has a number of important preceding factors which make up and contribute to the black child's self-image and feeling of self-worth. Logan[49] described them as:

> The role of the black family and its child-rearing practices, the absence or presence of the father, the nutritive or noxious aspects of the wider black community.

The role of the school

Like the family, the school plays an all-important role and is at the core of child development and identity formation. However, the school is the first place that the black child learns to hate him/herself. In order for children to achieve and value themselves the role of the school must be positive in so far as it can

> . . . control the conditions out of which deep-seated reactions spring . . . it can make contributions towards the emergence of a black self less prone to self-defeating behaviours and interactions.[50]

Thus schools are duty bound to provide the environment and learning climate that will encourage the black child to own his/her true identity and which will allow them to comfortably achieve their goals and aspirations.

The role of the black community

Barnes[51] argued that the concept of community is an important link in the development of identity. He placed emphasis on the interdependence of the black child and family with the community at large in so far as it supports group identity. The role of the community is to act as a buffer between the family and the wider society, reinforcing positive images of blackness.

Implications for black young people leaving care

It is important that professionals who work with black children recognise that the factor of "race" is an integral part of healthy development and positive identity. Logan[52] offers the following as a guide for those working with black children:

- willingness to rethink and reconceptualise the process through which development occurs (this should include physical maturation as well as life experiences);
- a concern for the variable of "race" and an understanding of intellectual and learning styles;
- an acceptance of black child studies as a unique and important area of human growth and development; and
- an acceptance of the colour black as a symbol of pride, worth and power.

Black children in care are at risk of losing their racial identity and their ability to connect with their own community after leaving care. A particular difficulty for black young people who are placed for adoption or in long-term foster care is that their placement might disrupt during the adolescent years. It is at these times that loss of racial identity is most striking.

The research of McRoy et al,[53] when examining racial identity, indicated that the children who had a positive identity were those who were encouraged to value their "race" and who were given positive feedback on their appearance. Some correlation was also found between positive racial identity and the environments within which the respondents lived. However, where the adoptive parents placed more emphasis on factors such as 'human identity, intelligence or hobbies' and discouraged the child from focusing on racial issues, there was a corresponding reluctance for these children to refer to themselves 'as belonging to a particular racial group'. What they found was that a high proportion of the families adopted a 'colour-blind approach to racial differences between the child and the family'. Significantly they all lived in predominantly white areas, and the children attended predominantly white schools. Racial differences were not discussed and the children viewed themselves as better than other black children.

References

1   Barker R and Moran M, *Workbook Prejudice and Abuse*, Open University, 1991.
2   Husbands C, *Race in Britain: Continuity and Change*, Hutchinson, 1982.
3   As 1 above.
4   Ahmad A, *Black Perspectives in Social Work*, Venture Press, 1990.
5   Thompson N, *Anti-discriminatory Practice*, Macmillan, 1993.
6   Penderhughes E, *Understanding Race, Ethnicity and Power: The key to efficacy in clinical practice*, Macmillan, 1989.
7   Ahmed S, Cheetham J, and Small J, *Social Work with Black Children and their Families*, BAAF/Batsford, 1989. Reprinted 1993.
8   Ezorsky G, *Racism and Justice: The case for affirmative action*, Cornell University Press, 1991, USA.
9   Dominelli L, *Anti-racist Social Work*, Macmillan, 1991. Reprinted 1994.
10 Hall S, Critcher C, Jefferson T, Clarke J and Roberts S, *Policing the Crisis: Mugging, the state, law and order*, MacMillan, 1978.
11 As 9 above.
12 As 4 above.
13 Coombe V, "Black Children in Residential Care", in Coombe V and Little A, *Race and Social Work*, Tavistock, 1988. Reprinted 1994.

14 Association of Black Social Workers and Allied Professionals (ABSWAP), *Black Children in Care*, Evidence to the House of Commons Social Services Committee, ABSWAP, 1983.

15 Fitzherbert K, *West Indian Children in London*, Bell and Sons, 1967.

16 Ely P and Denny D, *Social Work in a Multi-racial Society*, Gower, 1987.

17 As 9 above.

18 As 4 above.

19 Cheetham J (ed), *Social and Community Work in a Multi-racial Society*, Harper and Row, 1981.

20 As 2 above.

21 As 6 above.

22 Solomon B B, *Black Empowerment: Social work in oppressed communities*, Columbia University, 1976, USA.

23 As 16 above.

24 Nobles W, *Africanity and the Black Family: The development of a theoretical model*, Black Family Institute, 1985.

25 Haviland W, *Cultural Anthropolology*, Holt, Rinehart and Winston, 1978.

26 Chimezie A, "Theories of Black Culture", *Journal of Black Studies* 7, 216–228, 1983.

27 Ahmed S, "Black Children in Day Nursery: Some issues of practice", in Ahmed S, Cheetham J and Small B T (eds), *Social Work with Black Children and their Families*, Batsford, 1986. Reprinted 1993.

28 As 16 above.

29 Cheetham J, *Social Services for Ethnic Minorities in Britain and the USA*, Research Dissertation, Oxford, 1981.

30 As 15 above.

31 Wilson A, *The Developmental Psychology of the Black Child*, African Research Publications, 1980.

32 As 6 above.

33 Department of Health and Social Security, *Review of Child Care Law*, HMSO, 1985.

34 Maluccio A, Krieger R and Pine B, *Adolescents and their Preparation for Life after Foster Family Care*, CWLA, 1996, USA.

35 Frost N and Stein M, *Working with Young People Leaving Care*, HMSO, 1995.

36 White J and Parham T, *The Psychology of Blacks*, Prentice-Hall International, 1990.

37 Barnes F, "The black community as a source of positive self-concept for black children: A theoretical perspective", in Jones R L (ed), *Black Psychology*, 3rd edition, 1991.

38 Tajfel H, "Social identity and intergroup behaviour", in *Social Science Information* 13:2, 65–93, 1974.

39 Tizard B and Phoenix A, "Black identity and transracial adoption", *New Community* 15:3, 427–437, 1989.

40 Banks N, *"Techniques for direct identity work with black children"*, Adoption & Fostering, 16:3 19–24, 1992.

41 Harowitz R, "Racial aspects of self-identification in nursery school children", *Journal of Psychology* 7:8, 91–99, 1939.

42 Clark K, and Clark M, "The development of consciousness of self and the emergence of racial identification in negro pre-school children", in Newcomb and Hartley E (eds), *Readings in Social Psychology*, 1939.

43 Goodman M E, *Race Awareness in Young Children*, Collier, 1964.

44 Milner D, *Children and Race*, Penguin, 1975.

45 Erikson E, *Identity Crisis and Youth*, Norton,1968.

46 Logan S, "Race identity and black children in social casework", *Journal of Contemporary Social Work*, January 1981.

47 Gill O and Jackson B, *Adoption and Race: Asian and mixed-race children in white families*, Batsford, 1983.

48 Watson J, *Between Two Cultures: Migrants and minorities in Britain*, Blackwell, 1977.

49 As 46 above.

50 See 46 above.

51 As 37 above.

52 As 46 above.

53 McRoy R, Zurcher L, Lauderdale L and Anderson R, "The identity of transracial adoptees", *Social Casework* 651, 34–39, January 1984.

The study

Aims of the study

This study aims to do the following:
- understand the personal experiences of a small group of young black people who had been in local authority care;
- examine what relationships, if any, may exist between their ethnicity and their care experience; and
- present the findings of this research with a view to improving provision for young black people in local authority accommodation.

The research sites

The study was conducted in two local authorities in England; for the purpose of retaining confidentiality, these are referred to as Departments A and B. I worked in Department A and experienced limited problems in gaining access to local teams. The young people from black and minority ethnic groups were identifiable as information on ethnicity was recorded in accordance with the department's policy.

Access to Department B was negotiated at a fairly early stage in the research process, and was due largely to the researcher's prior links with a senior manager who readily gave permission for the research to take place. A request was made for allocated social workers to make initial approaches and explain the purposes of the study to the young people, thereby presenting them with enough information to enable them to make an informed choice about whether or not to participate. Following this, arrangements were made to meet the young people to describe the process of the research to them.

Most of the young people, with the exception of two, willingly gave their consent to participate in the study.

The sample

The sample consisted of ten young black people who had either left care or who were in the process of doing so. All of the study sample had been placed in long-term care in the early 1970s. Of the sample, six were female and four were male. All of the young people were of African or African-Caribbean origin with five being of mixed heritage, ie. with one black and one white parent.

Methodology

This is an exploratory study that sought to elicit information on human experience and life events including considering feelings, perceptions and behaviour patterns. The methodology adopted for this study was "grounded theory" based on the work of Glaser and Strauss[1] and Strauss and Corbin.[2] Grounded theory was the method used to explain behavioural patterns and to place within an analytical and scientific framework the meaning that young black people gave to their experiences both while in care and upon leaving care. Its intent is to develop theory 'without a particular commitment to specific kinds of data, lines of research or theoretical interest'. This methodology was chosen because it offered the following options:
- It was capable of explaining behaviour patterns from which practical applications could be made; and
- It was useful in developing and generating theory.

Initially, two interview methods were considered: a survey with a structured questionnaire, and in-depth interviews with open-ended questions. A larger study would have been possible making the study capable of generalisations and inferences about the population. However, it was decided not to employ this method because, in trying to produce comparable information, the depth and complexity of the experiences could have been lost.

Individual in-depth interviews were selected as the preferred method as they would allow the widest possible exploration of views and behaviour patterns. My aim in interviewing the young people was to enable them to talk without constraint or inhibition and at length about their lives in a way that meant something to them. Individual interviews also encouraged interaction with the young people and enabled more open and forthright recounting of their stories.

The questionnaire

A semi-structured questionnaire was developed for the individual in-depth interviews, with open-ended questions. These helped to measure the intensity of the respondents' feelings and to identify lack of understanding. They covered four broad areas:
- the care experience;
- family background;
- preparation for leaving care; and
- ethnicity and culture.

The pilot study

A pilot study was conducted and provided the framework for the subsequent field work and procedure for the formal collection of data. The pilot study was extremely useful in that it not only allowed for pretesting of the interview schedule but also measured the extent to which the young people could respond effectively to the interviewer and the questions.

Data from casework files

Supporting documentation was also viewed. The purpose of viewing casework files was to discover to what extent issues of "race" and culture had been recognised and integrated as part of the casework process. The documents enabled the construction of Eco maps for each individual that identified links with their family and depicted the young person in relation to a network. The notes taken from the records were integrated within the analysis to strengthen points that were made by the young people.

Supplementary data

A decision was made to build into the design two interviews with social workers in senior management positions in each department. These individuals gave information on departmental policies regarding black children within local authority care. There was no attempt to analyse these interviews in the same way as the data for the young people; only general themes and observations are recorded in the findings.

References

1   Glaser B and Strauss A, *The Discovery of Grounded Theory*, Aldine, 1967.
2   Strauss A and Corbin J, *Basics of Qualitative Research: Grounded theory procedures and techniques*, Sade, 1990.

The case histories

This chapter provides a glimpse into the histories of the respondents who participated in the study. A brief pen portrait is presented of each young person in the study sample; all the names have been changed to preserve the anonymity that was promised.

Name:	**Cassie**
Age at interview:	**23**
Time in care:	**15 years**
Care leaving age:	**18**
Present status:	**Unemployed mother of two**

Cassie is quietly spoken and displays an eagerness to talk about her experiences of the care system. Her recall of past events is impressive, but her facial expressions and occasional lapses into silence indicate her time in care was a painful one.

Parental neglect led Cassie to be placed in residential care at the age of three. Her brother and two sisters followed. Her white mother and black father, who were married when Cassie entered care, divorced soon after. As a result, the local authority was granted a Care Order.

Cassie, who describes herself as 'black', went through multiple residential placements including a spell in a mental institution. When she was 16, Cassie was allowed to live temporarily with her father.

This pattern of inconsistency was also reflected in her schooling. She was expelled from school which meant that her formal education was limited. To halt this downward spiral, she was removed from mainstream education and placed in various institutions offering basic levels of education. But apart from some work experience, she has never been employed.

Now Cassie is struggling, unsupported, to care for her two children. She had some contact with her parents but this did not materialise into anything long term; her mother does not live locally and, she says, her father is not that supportive. Cassie has no choice but to adapt to her single parent status as her partner and father of her children is in prison.

Name:	**Donneth**
Age at interview:	**24**
Time in care:	**6 years**
Care leaving age:	**18**
Present status:	**Single mother**

Donneth is strong, assertive and proud to be black. She has resolutely held on to her Caribbean culture through cooking traditional West Indian dishes, and having friends from a similar cultural background. But this personal confidence has roots in a painful and difficult past.

At the age of six months, Donneth was abandoned by her mother and left on the doorstep of an aunt. Her African-Caribbean parents subsequently divorced leaving Donneth to be brought up by her extended family. This was a disruptive period as no one adult was responsible for her care. The chance of a stable home life emerged when her father remarried. But Donneth's rejection of her step-mother's authority made living together impossible. By the age of 12 she was displaying challenging and disturbed behaviour which was affecting her performance at school. Donneth was also faced with the unexpected return of her mother, a woman she had never known.

Difficulties escalated as her mother attempted to reassert her parental authority after an eleven-year absence. Unfortunately, no meaningful relationship was established between them. Instead, the situation deteriorated to such a degree that the mother made death threats on Donneth's life. At 14 Donneth was placed on a Place of Safety Order by the local authority after which it was decided that she remain in care. During this time she was expelled from school without any qualifications.

Initially Donneth was placed with foster parents and then in a range of residential establishments. But her time in care was peppered with delinquent behaviour. She abused substances and was involved in criminal activity for which she received a custodial sentence.

At 15, while in care, she also became pregnant. The baby, a girl, was taken into care and never returned to Donneth. Acutely aware of her own unhappy care experience, she asked for her daughter to be placed with her godmother.

Several years later, after Donneth had left care and had two more children, she tried, unsuccessfully, to get her daughter back. Donneth claims that the local authority had formed an alliance with her godmother and together they worked against her application for contact and full custody. Since then, Donneth has had two more children and lives in council accommodation. Her relationship with her mother has never improved. But against all the odds she is coping well as a single mother and receives regular support from her extended family. There is one battle that Donneth is still fighting through the courts – to be a mother to her 'lost daughter'.

CASE	Name:	**Mark**
STUDY	Age at interview:	**19**
	Time in care:	**17 years**
THREE	Care leaving age:	**18**
	Present status:	**Student**

Ambitious, polite and softly spoken, Mark believes that he will make a success of his life. Verbally, he is very decisive and firm in his views and attitudes. His interest in sports is evident from his athletic frame and is reinforced through his work at a local sports centre during the college holidays.

Mark entered care when he was, in his own words, 'small'. He was 22 months old. Of mixed heritage – a white mother and African-Caribbean father – he was the subject of a Care Order and placed with white foster carers.

During the early years of his childhood, he had minimal contact with his mother and no contact with his father. Nevertheless, he developed a strong and affectionate bond with his foster parents. Living in a predominantly white area, Mark did not socialise with black children or adults either at school or in the local community. During his time in care, little reference was made to his racial identity and he adopted the cultural norms and values of his white foster family.

When Mark was at junior school age, contact with his birth mother was sporadic. At one point he actively refused to see her. However, he later asked for contact to be re-established, but this did not materialise. By this stage the local authority and Mark's foster parents agreed that contact with his mother was not in his best interests. It was concluded that his mother's intermittent visits were too disruptive and unsettling, leading to her rights of contact being terminated.

The local authority encouraged Mark's foster parents to apply for an adoption order which was rejected by the courts. When Mark was 12 they made a successful application for custodianship.

Mark asserts that the local authority did not adequately prepare him for independent living once he left care. Also, he points out, he failed to receive any specific support or counselling in relation to his racial identity or as a child in care.

Name:	**Tony**
Age at interview:	**16**
Time in care:	**14 years**
Care leaving age:	**18**
Present status:	**Young offender**

Tony's gentle nature and quiet voice contrast greatly with his large, muscular frame. He is conscious that his size occasionally makes people afraid of him. When he talks, his concentration wavers and he finds it difficult to focus his thoughts. Words do not come easily to Tony. A history of blocking out the pain in his life is a major factor behind his communication difficulties.

Neglect at the hands of a drug abusing mother led Tony to be taken into care at the age of four. The relationship between his white mother and black African father broke down after his birth because of his mother's drug abuse. Before he was taken into care he lived with an aunt and then his grandmother. Both placements broke down. He then lived with his musician father who was unable to cope.

This trend of family breakdown continued with his foster placements. His life was intensely unhappy and unsettled. This consistent lack of family stability and security during his childhood manifested itself through behavioural difficulties at school.

After a referral to the educational psychological services he was categorised as having special needs. Often, he ran away from home and played truant from school which led to exclusion. He was sent back to live with his mother on a trial basis. At this time he was stealing food from grocery stores to feed himself. A pattern of criminal activity emerged and, by the time Tony was 14, had become a serious problem which led to a custodial sentence.

Racial identity was another issue that had not been tackled and Tony often felt 'singled out' at school or by the police. He slowly began to link this sometimes hostile treatment to the colour of his skin. Tony lived in a predominantly white area with little or no contact with black people. As he had contact mostly with his white extended family and white foster carers he defined himself as white.

By the time he was 16 Tony was living with his aunt as a lodger though in keeping with the terms of his Care Order. There is no evidence to suggest that adoption was ever considered in his case. Although he was still in the care of the local authority, he was not receiving any after care support or preparation for independent living. Despite his unstable life and lack of qualifications, he had wanted to join the army but felt that his criminal record would go against him.

At the time of interview, Tony was still living with his aunt but had offences outstanding. He was subsequently imprisoned.

CASE	Name:	**Marcel**
STUDY	Age at interview:	**18**
	Time in care:	**11 years**
FIVE	Care leaving age:	**18**
	Present status:	**Drama school student**

Marcel's exuberance, confidence and determination are difficult to ignore. Able to express her opinions clearly, she comes across as a highly capable young woman, yet her confusion over her racial identity is never far away from the surface.

Born in Nigeria, Marcel emigrated to England with her mother (a divorcee) and younger sister when she was seven years old. Almost immediately she and her sister were privately fostered and lived with three different sets of white carers in different parts of England.

Local authority supervision of Marcel and her sister's care (while in private foster care) had been minimal. The risks of this situation became apparent when Marcel and her sister became homeless and were abandoned when their elderly white carer was evicted from her rented accommodation. Their mother, who had maintained contact with her children, offered them a home which they both rejected. According to Marcel, she had a strong disregard for her mother and the area in which she lived. The area in question was largely populated with people from African-Caribbean and other minority ethnic communities. This rejection of racial heritage was a common theme throughout Marcel's care experience.

White school officials and adults supported Marcel's decision not to return to her mother's care and convinced her that, if she did, she would be swiftly returned to Nigeria. Records from planning meetings bear this out and show that this fear was used by the local authority to take precipitous action.

Wardship applications were made and granted in the local authority's favour, giving them care and control over Marcel and her sister. The lack of same-race placements and Marcel and her sister's refusal to live with black carers meant they were placed in white foster homes. The impact of the decision meant that for the first time in her life, Marcel was separated from her sister which she found very traumatic.

Although Marcel had intermittently visited her mother over the years, her anger at her mother was deep and disturbing. She claims she had been physically abused by her and dismissed her African culture and origins by referring to the fact that she was 'brought up' by white families. In Marcel's eyes, she was white.

After completing her GCSEs the local authority financially assisted her to attend drama school. Although this settlement seemed to be part of her leaving care package, Marcel points out she did not receive any preparation for her move to independence and had no idea what the local authority's responsibilities for leaving care were.

CASE
STUDY
SIX

Name:	**David**
Age at interview:	**19**
Time in care:	**18 years**
Care leaving age:	**18**
Present status:	**Convicted prisoner**

Despite facing a long prison sentence and an uncertain future, David is surprisingly relaxed and willing to talk openly about his life in care. He is full of good humour and possesses an endearing personality. Yet the care path that led him to prison is one filled with abuse, rejection and violence. David's connection with the care system was cemented almost from birth. At the age of one month he came to the local authority's attention when his father abused him. Although the subject of a Place of Safety Order under the Children and Young Persons Act 1969, he was still returned to his parents, a white English mother and African-Caribbean father.

By the age of six months he had been taken into care following serious neglect by his mother. He and his sister were then adopted by a white couple living in an all-white suburb where they had no contact with black people. David was subsequently physically abused by his adoptive parents which led to his return to the care system. But the nightmare had not ended. While in a residential home, he was abused by a staff member. No support was forthcoming. Instead he was worryingly moved from one residential placement to another.

With each move, David became more rootless, disturbed and aggressive. Over time he became virtually unmanageable. His care records show clear signs of psychological trauma stemming from his early abusive experiences. Attempts to manage his challenging behaviour through placements in Community Homes with education and socio-therapeutic units failed. Labelled as maladjusted, he was expelled from junior school. From this point on he never gained a significant foothold in education.

David's racial identity was only addressed when he was 14 years old. That was when he requested to be sent to a black-run residential project for young black people. Somehow, he managed to develop a significant relationship with a black couple who became his informal support and he responded to them positively.

But contact with his birth family was virtually nonexistent. He was, in his view, well and truly institutionalised. When he left care he was unable to cope. The only real family he had was his sister who had also been abused by the adoptive parents. Her care history was unimpressive; she became an underage mother and had regular contact with the police. At the time of interview, David had limited contact with her.

No formal attempt was made to appropriately prepare David for leaving care. But he had had the benefit of living, albeit briefly, in a preparation unit at a children's home. Afterwards he went to live with a family as a lodger, an arrangement which soon broke down. His next home was a self-contained flat with a resident landlord, but he was unable to cope with independent living.

His survival in the community was short lived as he was arrested and detained in custody and is now serving a long-term prison sentence. He says that the only way he can live is in an institution. That is all he knows.

CASE	Name:	**Denzil**
STUDY	Age at interview:	**20**
	Time in care:	**17 years**
SEVEN	Care leaving age:	**18**
	Present status:	**Plasterer**

Denzil is shy, self-conscious and slightly hesitant. His apparent difficulty in understanding the questions forces me to repeat and reframe them for him to answer comfortably; the presence of his young cousin during the interview is also distracting. Denzil's parents – both from the Caribbean – divorced and he was then taken into care. Unable to cope with two children, his mother had approached the local authority for help. While in voluntary care, he went through a number of short-term foster placements. When a Care Order was granted, Denzil was placed with his aunt who had been approved as his foster carer under the Boarding Out Regulations. She acted as his main carer during most of his childhood with financial support from the local authority. Contact with social workers was minimal. He had companionship in the shape of his three cousins.

When Denzil was 13 his aunt had a baby and things started to go wrong. Feeling a strong sense of rejection he began to misbehave which culminated in unmanageable behaviour. His behaviour at school led to a suspension and then expulsion. Despite his admission to another school, he did not gain any qualifications. He was finally placed in residential care – first a children's home and then an Observation and Assessment Centre.

Following a period of assessment he was returned to the care of his aunt. However, the situation soon deteriorated when he started to commit petty offences. This time he was remanded to the care of the local authority, returned to the Observation and Assessment Centre and then placed in a community home.

When Denzil was 16, his persistent offending resulted in an eleven-month sentence at a remand centre. His aunt remained loyal to him and kept regular contact with him along with assurances that once he was released he could return to live with her. He also had contact with a social worker whom he regularly wrote to. Overall, Denzil's link with social services was tenuous as he always viewed his aunt as the main source of support.

Thankfully, his internment acted as an effective deterrent from committing further offences. His behaviour improved dramatically, leading to a good report on his release, and enabled him to look for employment.

Through sheer determination and persistence, Denzil found a full-time job as a plasterer. He is still living with his aunt as a lodger.

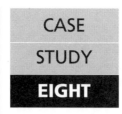

CASE

STUDY

EIGHT

Name:	**Natalie**
Age at interview:	**19**
Time in care:	**17 years**
Care leaving age:	**18**
Present status:	**Unemployed**

Her infectious laugh and glowing personality mean that Natalie is not someone you easily forget. Though nervous at times, she is very talkative, expressive and displays a maturity beyond her years. She is desperate to tell her story to help other young black people in care who may be struggling to find themselves as she did.

Natalie was born to African-Caribbean parents and was largely in the care of her mother. Until the age of two, she was regularly separated from her mother and admitted to day nurseries and short-term foster care placements. These separations had a damaging effect on her personal development.

The situation led the local authority to seek a legal order on the ground that her mother's care was unsatisfactory and not serving Natalie's best interests. Although her mother fought hard to keep Natalie, she found it extremely difficult to cope with her daughter's severe eczema and asthma. Once the local authority secured a Care Order, Natalie – still aged two – was placed with white foster parents. There were some serious drawbacks to the placement. When she was put in their care, the foster parents were childless and already close to retirement age. They had little or no contact with black people and during Natalie's childhood made no attempt to become involved with the black community. Yet they had a long history of fostering black children. A request by her birth mother that Natalie be adopted was ignored.

Despite all the drawbacks of the placement, Natalie remained with the family until she was 16. It later came to light that she had a number of relatives but she had lost contact with them as well as with her mother. Her care records show that contact with her birth mother had not been encouraged by her foster parents. They argued that the mother reminded them that they were not Natalie's real parents and that Natalie was black.

In her early teens, Natalie searched for her family to compensate for her gnawing sense of loss and isolation. She initiated a covert and secret process of contact with them. At that time the incoming social worker was expected to complete work with Natalie on her birth family and carry out life story work to enable open contact with her relatives to put an end to the secret assignations.

Following the breakdown of her foster placement she moved in with her boyfriend's parents and through her own efforts got in contact with her mother.

Natalie states that she was not given any preparation for leaving care such as budgeting, advice on paying bills and claiming benefits. At the time she didn't have any idea what leaving local authority care would mean in practice. She was consumed with feelings of dread and fear at having to face the world on her own.

CASE STUDY NINE	Name:	**Sandra**
	Age at interview:	**18**
	Time in care:	**18 years**
	Care leaving age:	**18**
	Present status:	**Unemployed**

Although on the surface Sandra appears quiet and shy, I am left with an underlying feeling that this is not her true persona. Her initial reluctance to talk soon dissolves and she becomes more animated, offering interesting and insightful perceptions about her life. With some perseverance and patience I gradually win her confidence which, considering her life history, is no small achievement.

Sandra's life was blighted from birth. When she was born, both her white English mother and black American father were in prison for the manslaughter of her sister at the age of 17 months. As Sandra was born in prison she was immediately removed from her mother's care and made a ward of court. Soon after a Care Order was made in favour of the local authority.

She was placed with white foster parents and when she was three years old the placement – at their request – was made permanent. However, within a year of this new arrangement it was discovered that Sandra was being emotionally abused. She was immediately removed and placed with alternative white foster parents.

By the age of nine Sandra began having difficulties. It soon came to light that she wasn't fully integrated into the family structure and her presence was resented by relatives of the foster family. Yet each child care review reported that the placement was progressing well.

There were no plans to rehabilitate Sandra with her mother, despite her release and legal attempts to regain parental responsibility. Having lost the legal battle, her mother returned to the USA.

When Sandra was ten she became withdrawn and found it hard to make friends. Bullying and victimisation were cited as some of the reasons for this shift in her behaviour. As her problems intensified, the local authority paid for her mother to come to England and visit. Then the authority paid for Sandra to see her mother in the USA.

When Sandra was 14, the foster placement irretrievably broke down leading Sandra into residential care. This decision exacerbated her problems. Although she had the potential to be a good student, her education continued to deteriorate. She played truant regularly and was constantly in difficulties with the police which resulted in her expulsion.

Sandra's potential has not been realised. She is unemployed and lives in a poorly maintained basement flat. Alienated from her family, she feels isolated and alone. The only assistance she received for leaving care was some help to get her present accommodation.

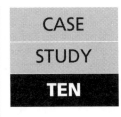

CASE

STUDY

TEN

Name:	**Paula**
Age at interview:	**18**
Time in care:	**4 years**
Care leaving age:	**18**
Present status:	**Living independently in own flat**

Paula comes across as a mature and decisive young woman. She finds it easy to communicate her thoughts and feelings effectively and shows a keen interest in African culture. Talking in her tastefully furnished flat, she is relaxed and proud of her independence.

Until the age of five Paula lived with her grandmother in Jamaica; her parents had emigrated to England. By the time Paula came to England, her parents had divorced, her mother had remarried and there were new siblings to contend with. As soon as mother and daughter were reunited there were problems. Paula's relationship with her mother and new family was so poor that they were referred to the Child and Family Clinic for therapeutic support.

As far as the parents were concerned, the root of the difficulties were Paula's stealing and behavioural problems. Paula disagreed and argued that her mother did not love her and treated her like "a little housewife". Unfortunately, the clinic failed to avert a breakdown between Paula and her parents.

Such were the problems that when Paula was 13 she was admitted to an observation unit. It too failed to halt the declining relationship between mother and daughter. Paula's mother hinted that she would be "put into care". And at the end of the observation period her mother requested that she be placed in voluntary care on the grounds that she was beyond parental control.

During this period Paula threatened on a number of occasions to commit suicide which made it unsafe for her to return to the family home. Instead, she was made the subject of a Care Order and placed in a residential unit where she remained for four years and eight months.

A black social worker was assigned to her who, she says, was a positive influence during a troubled and painful transition in residential care. This sense of stability increased when she was referred to a leaving care unit. With the social worker's support, Paula's transition from care to living independently in a small flat, which she found herself, was relatively pain free. The few weeks of preparation for leaving care and financial support to acquire the flat has helped Paula begin her life of independence.

The findings

An analysis of the data forms the findings and includes excerpts from field notes and memos in diagrammatic form, where appropriate. Where possible, the data have been illustrated with quotes from the respondents.

A clear distinction has been made between where the participants' comments end and where the analysis begins. Whilst I have not concentrated on individuals, comparisons are made between the histories of the young people, and a number of statements are presented to illustrate congruence and common themes that are suffused within the data.

Questions were asked before the interview and elicited information of a general nature. Tables 1 to 6 show the responses given by each participant to questions based on the demographic questionnaire.

All the young people in this study had been on Care Orders and the majority had been in care virtually all their lives. It is significant to note that none of the young people reported major difficulties in finding accommodation. Yet only four were living independently after leaving care.

	Admission year	Age on leaving care	Total years in care
Cassie	1973	18 (home on trial at 16)	15
Donneth	1987	18	6
Mark	1976	18	17
Tony	1981	18	12
Marcel	1982	18	11
David	1974	18	18
Denzil	1975	18	17
Natalie	1976	18	17
Sandra	1975	18	18
Paula	1989	18	4

Table 1

Admission into care and total number of years in care

Name	Legal status	Placement type
Cassie	Care Order	FC/RC (multiple placements)
Donneth	Care Order	FC/RC (multiple placements)
Mark	Care Order	FC/Custodianship (one placement)
Tony	Care Order	FC with relatives (multiple placements)
Marcel	Care Order	PFC/FC (multiple placements)
David	Care Order	Adoption and RC (multiple placements)
Denzil	Care Order	FC and RC (limited placements)
Natalie	Care Order	FC (limited placements)
Sandra	Care Order	FC/RC (multiple placements)
Paula	Care Order	RC (limited placements)

Note: All placements are transracial.
FC = Foster Care; RC = Residential Care;
PFC = Private Foster Care.

Table 3

Qualifications on leaving care and plans for further study

	GCSEs	Engaged in further study
Cassie	No	No
Donneth	No	Yes
Mark	Yes	Yes
Tony	No	No
Marcel	Yes	Yes
David	No	No
Denzil	No	No
Natalie	Yes	Yes
Sandra	No	No
Paula	Yes	Yes

Note: Over 50 per cent of the participants left school without qualifications

	Description of "race" in care	Present description of "race"
Cassie	white	black
*Donneth	black	black
Mark	mixed heritage	white
Tony	white	black
Marcel	African	me
David	white	black
*Denzil	black	black
Natalie	white	African-Caribbean
Sandra	white	black
*Paula	black	black

*Experienced most time with birth or extended family

Table 4

Racial identity as defined by the sample

Note: All the young people experienced problems about their racial identity while in care except those whose entry into care had been delayed. An early and fixed sense of identity was crucial in maintaining racial identity, as was preserving cultural links with parents and relatives.

	Contact while in care	Present contact
Cassie	No	Yes
Donneth	Yes	Yes
Mark	Yes/No	No
Tony	Yes	Yes
Marcel	Yes	No
David	No	No
Denzil	Yes	Yes
Natalie	No	Yes
Sandra	No/Yes later	Yes
Paula	Yes	Yes

Table 5

Re-establishing contact with parents and relatives

Note: Seven out of ten maintained or re-established contact with parents and relatives. Significantly, those who did not accept a black identity (Mark and Marcel) did not have contact with their parents.

Table 6

Preparation for leaving care

Preparation for leaving care	Numbers of respondents
Help with accommodation	4
No help with accommodation	6
Placement converted to lodgings	4
Living in lodgings	1
Living alone (council accommodation)	4
Prison	1
Cash assistance	
Leaving care grant (cash)	2
Assistance with further education	2
No after care support	6
Preparation by foster carers or residential care staff	
Access to preparation units	2
Involved in preparation plans	0
Carers actively promoted preparation	0

Seven of the young people experienced problems over their racial identity. All were largely surrounded by white people during their childhood and some still are. Despite long periods of separation from their families, most of the young people managed to re-establish some form of contact with their parents and close relatives. Some of the long-term effects of separation on them were strong feelings of rejection and generally an impact on their mental health. These important factors impinged on the young people at the point of leaving care.

Analyses of the data are summarised in Tables 7 and 8. Important factors to note are:
a) A significant number of the respondents had experienced physical and emotional abuse; six out of ten reported some form of abuse or distress within the family unit. These factors led to reception into care.

b) All of the participants described themselves as having been rejected.

c) All of the participants had experienced transracial placements, and most had lived in areas that did not expose them to black people. This led to feelings of isolation and alienation, even if they were living in multiracial areas with white carers.

d) All the respondents reported racism at school and within their care setting, having limited or no help from carers and professionals to help with the stress and negative feelings left in the wake of racist behaviour. Significantly, six of the sample were excluded from mainstream education.

e) More than half the participants experienced excessive moves (ie. more than four), most of them several times and in two cases more than 12 times. This led to rootlessness and poor, fragmented care trajectories.

f) Six out of ten had been in residential care – only one had ever been placed for adoption – and none had been placed with a black foster family. Seven said that they wished they had been given the opportunity to live with a black family; the other three had already had this experience within their own extended family.

g) Seven reported problems with their racial identity which had been stripped away during the early stages of entering into care. This was a process that continued throughout care, augmented by restricted family contact. "Identity stripping" was also a major contributory factor in the loss of racial identity and culture. Table 7 shows that the maintaining of identity was directly linked to early positive experiences within the black family. Therefore those entering care at a later age were not as severely damaged and had their culture to sustain them. A lack of knowledge about family and confusion over personal history were reported by six out of the ten young people as "not knowing".

h) The concept of "identity unfolding" occurred at a late stage in the care trajectory. Although most of the respondents recognised that their racial identity had been stripped, only four allowed their identities to unfold. For some, this process had been irrevocable.

i) All had viewed being in care as shameful and negative and had felt stigmatised and powerless. This sense of intense powerlessness was drastically reduced for those who had the advantage of early family experiences. Most of the respondents expressed views relating to limited communication and had real problems in communicating with adults while in care.

j) In seven cases, the young people reported negative responses to the foster family and from the family to them as children in care. This was to greatly influence their perceptions of care. The care system was described as both 'caring and non caring', indicating a dichotomy within the care system and their own ambivalent feelings.

k) Eight of the young people said they had had no preparation for leaving care.

Table 7

Data analysis

	1	2	3	4	5	6	7	8	9	10	Totals
Abuse prior to care	Y	Y	Y	Y	N	Y	N	N	N	Y	6
Negative/control responses to family problems	Y	N	Y	Y	Y	Y	N	Y	Y	N	7
Feelings of rejection	Y	Y	Y	Y	Y	Y	Y	Y	Y	Y	10
Received into care as young children	Y	N	Y	Y	Y	Y	Y	Y	Y	N	8
Found care caring	N	Y	Y	N	Y	N	Y	N	N	Y	5
Found care non-caring	Y	Y	N	Y	N	Y	Y	Y	Y	N	7
Placed in transracial placements	Y	Y	Y	Y	Y	Y	Y	Y	Y	Y	10
Placed in multiracial area	N	N	N	N	N	N	Y	Y	N	Y	3
Wished I had been placed with a black family	Y	–	Y	Y/N	N	Y	–	Y	Y	–	6
Restricted or no family contact	Y	Y	Y	N	Y	Y	N	Y	Y	N	7
Poor education/excluded	Y	Y	N	Y	N	Y	Y	Y	Y	N	7
Faced racism at school	Y	Y	Y	Y	Y	Y	Y	Y	Y	Y	10
Faced racism in care	Y	Y	Y	Y	Y	Y	Y	Y	Y	Y	10

KEY
Y = Yes; N = No
– = Does not apply

Table 8

Data analysis

	1	2	3	4	5	6	7	8	9	10	Totals
Feelings of isolation	Y	Y	Y	Y	Y	Y	N/Y	Y	Y	N	8
Alienation and feelings of powerlessness	Y	Y	Y	Y	Y	Y	Y	Y	Y	N	9
Multiple movements	Y	Y	N	Y	Y	Y	N	N	Y	N	6
Offending behaviour	N	Y	N	Y	N	Y	Y	N	Y	N	5
Institutional care	Y	Y	N	N	N	Y	Y	N	Y	Y	6
Signs of rootlessness	Y	N	Y	Y	Y	Y	N	Y	Y	N	7
Identity stripping	Y	N	Y	Y	Y	Y	N	Y	Y	N	7
Identity unfolding	Y	N	N	N	N	Y	N	Y	Y	N	4
Confused over history	Y	N	Y	Y	N	Y	N	Y	Y	N	6
Prepared for leaving care in any way	N	N	N	N	N	N	Y	N	N	Y	2
Found care stigmatising	Y	Y	Y	Y	N	Y	N	Y	Y	Y	8
Communication problems	Y	N	Y	Y	Y	Y	N	Y	Y	N	7

The care experience – concerns and issues

Being placed in care

Rejection by birth parents was the first experience all the young people alluded to and attached meaning to. This was the time when they asked questions such as 'Who am I?' and 'Why am I in care?', which required some personal examination of the reasons leading up to their placement in care. Disruptive family experiences helped to reinforce feelings of abandonment and rejection. In the absence of explanations from carers and social workers the young people formed their own conclusions. Without exception, these were all negative.

It did seem to me that when I was a kid, I had been dumped somewhere. People didn't really care. (Natalie)

Why was I in a foster home? Didn't my parents want me? (Mark)

Mum didn't have time for me and my sister. I heard from someone, but I don't know if it's true, that my mum was a heroin addict. (David)

I thought my parents didn't like me no more. I was young, but when I got older I started to think that nobody cared anyway. (Cassie)

Disruption within marriage or partnership contributed to separation and fuelled the young person's sense of rejection.

In the first place my mum and dad had problems and that in their marriage, and then I think my mum wanted me to go into care because she couldn't cope with me. (Mark)

My nan told me that my mum was taking drugs and my dad couldn't put up with it, so they split up. My mum couldn't look after me so she put me in care. (Tony)

My mum wasn't married to my dad. She was married to another person, and I think it was that, that was at the beginning of it. She couldn't look after me properly. (Mark)

Donneth spoke vividly about the way she had been abandoned:

My mother disappeared off the face of the earth. Nobody knew where she was. She just disappeared and left me on my aunt's doorstep. (Donneth)

In Marcel's case, long-term private fostering from the age of two had similar detrimental effects. The strong sense of rejection was magnified by being uprooted from her black culture and being placed in a 'white culture'.

My mother all of a sudden wants me to be in a black culture, when she put me in a white culture anyway. (Marcel)

However valid the reasons for entry into care, the way it was felt, perceived and initially internalised was as outright rejection. Abuse within the family was another precipitating factor.

I used to get hit at home. I used to wet the bed a lot, and the more I did it, the more I got hit. Everything was left down to me. I was like a little housewife. (Paula)

For Cassie, a lack of supervision and parental care led to a lifetime in care. Her sense of reality and knowledge were based on limited information about the real reason she was placed in care.

I got told that the neighbour reported us to the social services, that we were left alone in the house. When the social services came there was no one in the house but us kids. (Cassie)

She was also angry and bitter about the way in which she was removed from her parents:

They should not have picked us up like that and thrown us into care. I didn't know what was going on. Being put in care and seeing my mother running down the road stuck in my mind. It will never go out of my mind. They should have tried and come round, tried to find out what the problem was, and try to stop putting a child in care. (Cassie)

These factors acted as determinants of the experience itself. The respondents often interpreted the reasons why they were in care in contradictory ways. For example, one young man recalled how his mother was unable to care for him. He admitted that he missed her a lot, but said that as he got older he could see what she was really like. Then he added: 'She's not bad really.'

The timing of entry into care

The second important component was timing – when the child entered care – and the significance of past, present and future experiences. The past encompassed incidents that occurred prior to entry into care, and all subsequent experiences arising out of the care episode. The present represented the here and now and how the young people understood and managed these experiences. The future related to leaving care and becoming independent adults. How much the young people knew about why they were placed in care was determined by the age at which that experience occurred. Most of the respondents admitted they had very little knowledge about the circumstances behind their admission into care.

I think there are secrets. I have never been told anything. (Natalie)

In the absence of accurate background information, most of the young people had to come to their own conclusions. Details that most children in a family would have access to, and which would be theirs by right, were withheld. For example, Mark was unaware that he was fostered and knew very little about the stigma attached to being in a foster family until he went to school.

When I was small I didn't really know about care or fostering until I was about eight, then I found out about fostering. Some kids would say you are fostered, and I would get upset about it. When you are young you look at other kids and see what they have got, and sometimes I couldn't have those things. Also the kids used to say, 'Where is your mum? Where is your dad?' And I would say 'I don't know'. Sometimes I would lie about it by saying 'my mum's here, my dad's there'. (Mark)

The age when the young people came into care had a direct influence on identity, self-knowledge and understanding. Age also determined the nature of the experience, what it felt like and how negative feelings were internalised and understood. Natural feelings of missing their parents coupled with an inability to understand the concept of separation were the result of this process.

> I used to miss my mum a lot when I was younger. I missed my dad but I hardly ever saw my dad. I didn't see my dad at all because he was so far away. (Mark)

The length of time a young person was in care had a direct bearing on how feelings of separation were internalised and perceived and how they tried to make sense of the experience. Perception of events was also affected by how young they were at the time of admission.

> Well, I've been fostered since I was two years old I think. Oh, it's so hard because I don't really know much about my life. I only remember what my foster parents have told me because my real mum changes her mind every week about how long I was in Nigeria and how long I was fostered. As far as I know I was fostered from when I was two years old. (Marcel)

When asked if he had ever lived with his parents, Tony said:

> I did, but I was too young to remember. I don't remember either of them.

Early separation usually led to estrangement, a lack of parental contact and feelings of loss. Before long anger and anxiety emerged.

> I don't really care anymore. When I was younger my mum used to come and see me, but as I got older she hasn't really bothered. She is supposed to come and see me at Christmas and stuff, but she doesn't bother. She doesn't send me birthday cards or anything, so in my view I haven't got a mother anymore. If my friends say 'Have you got a mum?' I say 'no', cause I just don't bother with her. She don't bother with me, so I don't care about her. (Mark)

After a few years in care, the whole situation was reinterpreted as normality.

> I've never really thought about it. It seems normal to me. I've been in care as long as I can remember so it don't make no difference. (Tony)

Tony's inability to recall past events was supplemented by his care records. They showed a history of abuse. In care, his emotional abuse continued as he was regularly moved, creating a sense of instability. Remembering these events was contextualised within the scope of timing. As his time in care was prolonged, his power of recall diminished.

Delving into the past can bring to the fore memories that are too painful to confront. Many of the respondents were reminded of being rejected by their parents. Others remembered care as just a bureaucratic system. Trying to remember often highlighted the absence of the love and support of the family.

Under what conditions was timing important?

Timing appeared to be most important when the young people entered care. The younger they were, the longer they remained. This increased the potential for them to languish in care without any concrete long-term placement plans. All these factors had an impact on their movement and the strategies adopted to control and administer what was perceived as care. The earlier the age of entry and the longer the time in care, the greater the negative effects on self-image, particularly in terms of ethnic and cultural identity. Eight of the young people in this study entered care early on in their childhood and were not discharged until the age of 18.

Age at the time of entry into care and duration in care affected the level of parental contact and depth of knowledge about their ethnic and cultural heritage. The younger they were at the time of coming into care, the more tenuous were their links with their cultural heritage. A combination of factors, ranging from disruption in the structure of the family to total breakdown, precipitated their entry into care. Marital conflict, separation and divorce were common themes. There was also parental failure to cope or to exert control over their children's disturbed and, in some cases, offending behaviour.

Poor recall of events prior to the young people's entry into care was not all down to the parents. File records showed no evidence that any life story work was carried out by social workers. To compensate, independent and personal conclusions had been drawn from informal sources, but the young people were never confident about the accuracy of the information received. A common response to any question about their past was, 'I don't know'.

> I've heard bits and bobs, but I still don't know . . . My mum says to me it was my dad's fault. My mum said that my dad couldn't look after me so he put me in care, that's what my mum said. But then my nan told me that my mum was taking drugs and my dad couldn't put up with it, so they split up. My mum couldn't look after me, so she put me in care. I've got different stories at the moment. (Tony)

> Well I don't know all the story at the moment, because my mum hasn't told me anything. No one has ever told me. No one ever knew, my mother kept it private from my family. (Natalie)

Contact with parents and relatives are vital links for young children and the lack of meaningful and consistent contact can be harmful. Those who had entered care as babies or toddlers had less contact with their parents. This limited or non-existent contact added to the already strong feelings of rejection which intensified over time.

> My mum used to come and see me. I used to get on with her and she used to come and see me a couple of times. When I was younger she used to come and see me a lot. As I got older she hasn't bothered. (Mark)

Lost contact resulted in displaced identity. The age at which the young people came into care had a significant impact on the level of appreciation and knowledge about their cultural roots.

> Well, the first thing is that you definitely lose contact with your roots a lot. You lose your contact with black people. I didn't have that much contact when I was with the foster parents . . . I had no contact, but my family was trying to look for me, and then there was me looking for

them. They thought I was lifted off the face of the earth. My aunt looked after me when I was little and all of a sudden I just disappeared. (Natalie)

The problems the young people faced within their families were replaced or reinforced when they entered care. This realisation reinforced their feelings of rejection. For example, David and Denzil were both abused by their families. Once in care they were physically, emotionally and racially abused.

One thing that was really important when I lived with my adoptive parents is they used to beat me. At a residential home, there was a guy called Mr Brown [alias]. The place has closed down so it's irrelevant. But this guy used to beat up young kids all the time. A lot of the staff did, the police are usually on their side because they are older. (David)

These negative experiences in care raised serious questions over whether the young people needed to be separated from their parents and family on a long-term basis. Those who entered care when they were older had different experiences. Denzil, Donneth and Paula are examples.

Figure 1 shows David's care history. His care trajectory is dominated by excessive movements and institutionalisation. It started with a move from an abusive family to the care system. He experienced failed foster placements, a disruption of a transracial adoption followed by a series of movements within residential units and educational institutions. This eventually led to offending behaviour and incarceration during and beyond leaving care. The trajectories of Tony and David show a series of movements leading to fragmented lives. Movement led to instability and negative experiences. Whether the movement occurred within the immediate family or the care system, the end result was negative and damaging. Donneth, Denzil and Paula had remained within their respective families until they were older. Their experience contrasted with David's. They were able to maintain their black culture, had a strong sense of racial identity, and had family networks they could tap into once in care. It helped that they were old enough to initiate contact themselves, knew the values of black family life and could express their wishes and follow them through.

Figure 2 shows that Paula experienced early separation from her parents, but contact was maintained with the extended family until the age of 13. It was not until resources within the family had been exhausted that institutional care became an option. Paula was involved in this decision because of her age. A limited number of movements resulted in a more postive outcome.

Likewise, Denzil's care trajectory, as shown in Figure 3, illustrates a less complicated picture. This was directly influenced by the fact he remained with his family until aged 13. Once in care, contact with the family was sustained. Its effectiveness led to less movement and positive relations with his family.

Coming into care could not be seen as the panacea for problem-solving. It presented its own conflicts and contradictions.

Actually, I went into care at 13. It made me grow up quickly. It made me grow up streetwise and stuff. (Paula)

Late entry into care was noted as having particular advantages for Donneth, such as being more aware of "race", culture, family and being in care.

David's care history

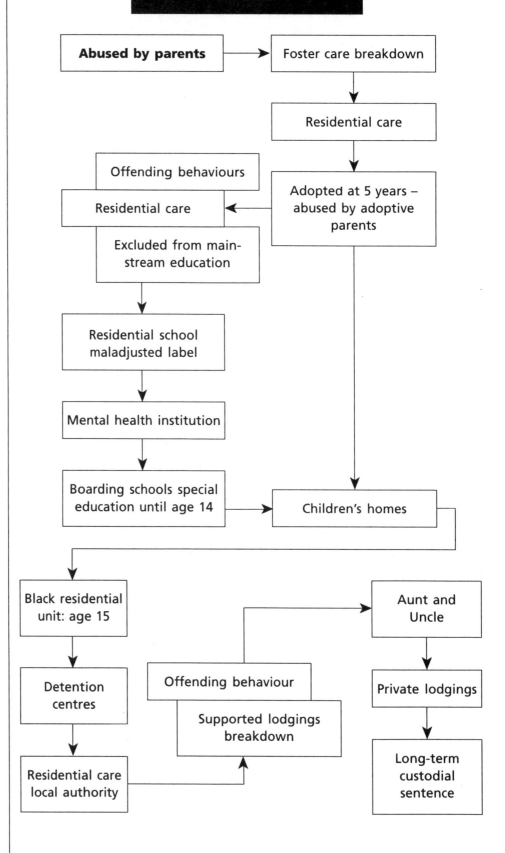

Movement and disruption in care

Abused by parents	Foster care breakdown

Residential care

Offending behaviours

Residential care

Adopted at 5 years – abused by adoptive parents

Excluded from main-stream education

Residential school maladjusted label

Mental health institution

Boarding schools special education until age 14

Children's homes

Black residential unit: age 15

Detention centres

Offending behaviour

Supported lodgings breakdown

Aunt and Uncle

Private lodgings

Residential care local authority

Long-term custodial sentence

David's care trajectory was dominated by movement and abuse.

Paula's care history

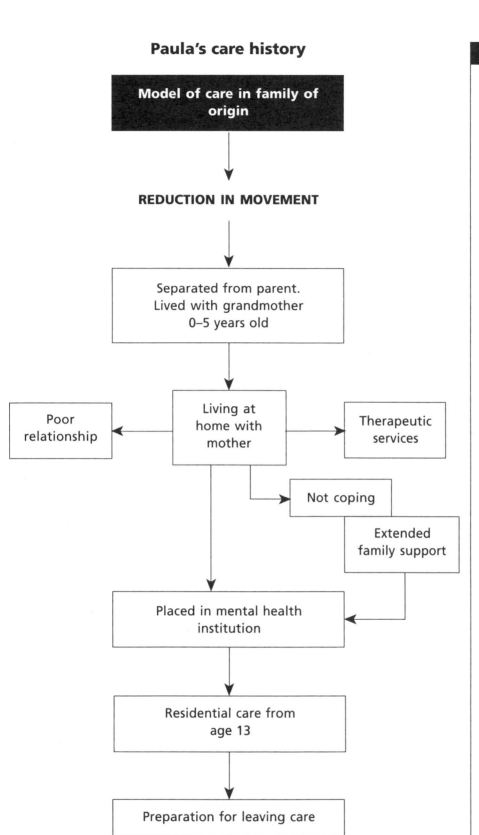

Model of care in family of origin

↓

REDUCTION IN MOVEMENT

↓

Separated from parent.
Lived with grandmother
0–5 years old

↓

Poor relationship ← Living at home with mother → Therapeutic services

→ Not coping

Extended family support

Living at home with mother ↓ Placed in mental health institution ← Extended family support

↓

Residential care from age 13

↓

Preparation for leaving care

↓

Move to own lodgings

Maintenance within the extended black family coupled with reduction in movement resulted in a positive outcome for Paula.

Figure 2

Figure 3

Denzil's care history

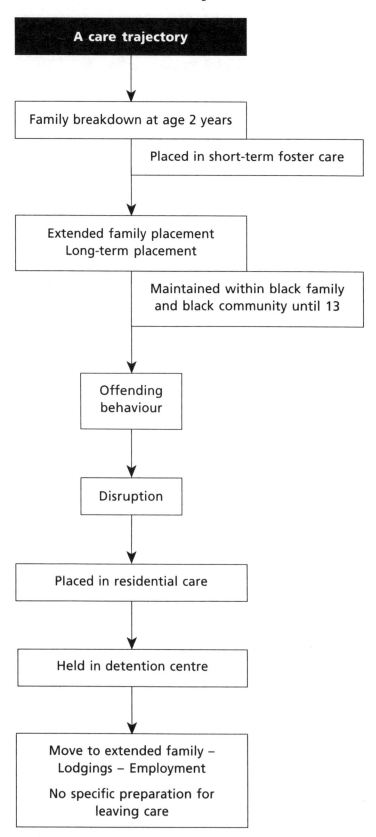

A care trajectory

Family breakdown at age 2 years

Placed in short-term foster care

Extended family placement
Long-term placement

Maintained within black family
and black community until 13

Offending
behaviour

Disruption

Placed in residential care

Held in detention centre

Move to extended family –
Lodgings – Employment

No specific preparation for
leaving care

This diagram shows although Denzil was on a Care Order from the age of two he had a qualitatively different concept of self to those in transracial placements. Significant to his trajectory is the reduction in movements.

My advantage was as a black person I had my family before going into care. So I knew about cooking and the way black people live their lives. But for those of them who are in care and don't know, it's hard when they leave. (Donneth)

Being able to make a decision on the level and regularity of contact was clearly an advantage.

I have links with all my family, aunties, uncles and gran. I see all of them. When I was in the children's home I used to visit them all. My family did not want me to go to a children's home. (Paula)

Movement as a sub-category of timing

When the care trajectories of the young people are compared they show a common theme of movement throughout a prolonged period in foster care and/or residential care. These patterns suggest that the continuous movement of young people increased the potential of a negative outcome. However, where there was extended family contact and delayed entry into care, the young people expressed less negative views and feelings about the effects of care on their self-image – a pattern that emerged in the trajectories of Donneth, Paula and Denzil. In the case of Tony (see Figure 4) who lived with his white extended family, there was a dominant pattern of movement, instability, and poor self-image. A similar pattern applied to Cassie, Marcel, David and Sandra.

For those who remained with their extended family, the level and quality of care and reduced movement gave them a stronger racial identity, and positive feelings about family and being part of a wider black community. There was also a consciousness about the significance of skin colour and a recognition of the family's role in maintaining and sustaining their culture. Leaving their families was viewed as 'hard' and led to what was described by one respondent as 'streetwise maturity'. There was another category – young people who had been in long-term care but had access to stability through reduced movement. Despite being in transracial placements, Mark and Natalie experienced consistency in their care trajectories. Nonetheless, they developed major problems over racial identity. This study found that when a young person was kept either within the family or extended family there was a more positive outcome both in the development of a stronger identity and cultural awareness. Therefore, reduction in movement had clear benefits.

When movement occurred within the family or in care it reinforced a young person's ambivalent feelings over their care experience. Strong feelings of being disliked and devalued were evident.

When I was young I thought my parents didn't like me anymore. But when I got older I started to think that nobody cared anyway. (Cassie)

Similarly, Donneth later became acutely aware of the negative impact of her early experiences, especially the number of times she was moved within her extended family and then in care.

Every time an argument built up and and exploded between me and my stepmother, my dad would say, 'Right! Send her to her grandad or send her to aunty'. I've never stayed in one place for more than a year. I was constantly moving around. (Donneth)

Tony's care history

Figure 4

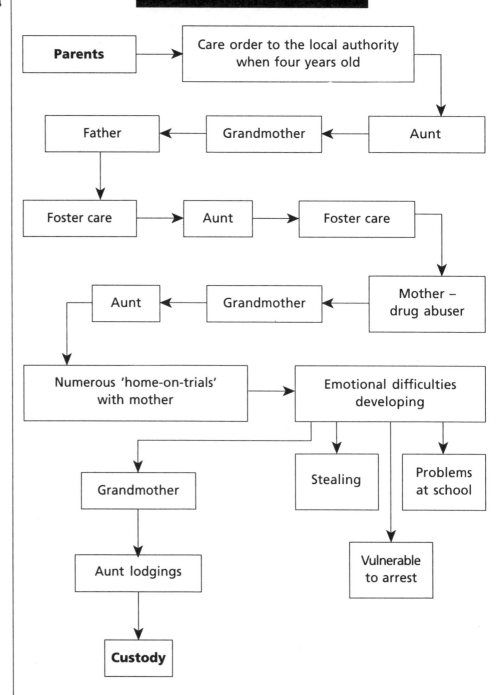

Movements in care within the extended family

Parents → Care order to the local authority when four years old

Father ← Grandmother ← Aunt

Father → Foster care → Aunt → Foster care

Foster care → Mother – drug abuser

Aunt ← Grandmother ← Mother – drug abuser

Aunt → Numerous 'home-on-trials' with mother → Emotional difficulties developing

Emotional difficulties developing → Grandmother

Emotional difficulties developing → Stealing

Emotional difficulties developing → Problems at school

Stealing → Vulnerable to arrest

Grandmother → Aunt lodgings → **Custody**

Although Tony remained in his white extended family, lack of permanence and frequent movement resulted in a poor care history.

Within the care setting "movement" was interpreted as the way powerful adults rendered children powerless. It made them feel controlled and without any rights. These feelings were summarised by some young people as 'I was put' or 'I got moved'.

> *When they couldn't cope with me, they went and put me in an adolescent unit. When I first saw the place, I thought why did they put me in a mental institution? I'm not mad. I'm not crazy. But you end up thinking like that.* (Cassie)

Considering that these children were placed into care because they were vulnerable, the care system did not provide a better alternative.

> *I was getting out of control and I misbehaved badly. The staff couldn't cope with me no more, so they thought it was a good idea if I went to another institution.* (Donneth)

Movement was linked by the young people to control. Institutional care was presented to them as the only and the best solution.

> *I was sent to foster parents, and I was sent to children's homes. I was sent to my mum's, but things didn't go to plan. I left again and ended up at the ABC home. I left ABC and got put into D house.* (Donneth)

The twin themes of powerlessness and lack of control emerged at a fairly early stage in the analysis. They indicated how the young people reflected on their care experiences and coped with the feelings they produced. Feelings of powerlessness were reinforced by various adult–child relationships such as abuse situations, a lack of choice, excessive movement and limited opportunities for self-determination.

Submerged, but integral to the care experience, were feelings of loss, sadness, estrangement and rejection. These produced conflicting and contradictory responses to their experiences. Many who spent long periods in care were in denial about the pain and sadness they felt. In order to cope they blanked these feelings out. Figure 5 illustrates how a feeling of powerlessness affected the young people's perception of self.

Caring and non-caring

During the initial stages of the study a category was developed to consider aspects of caring and non-caring. It was used to follow up the meaning the young people gave to the care experience. The major questions asked of the data were:

1) What were the meanings given by the young people to their "care" experience?
2) What were the conditions under which they experienced care as "caring" and "non-caring", and what words described their feelings about these conditions?
3) What strategies did they develop to cope with the feelings and pain associated with the event?
4) What were the consequences for these young people?

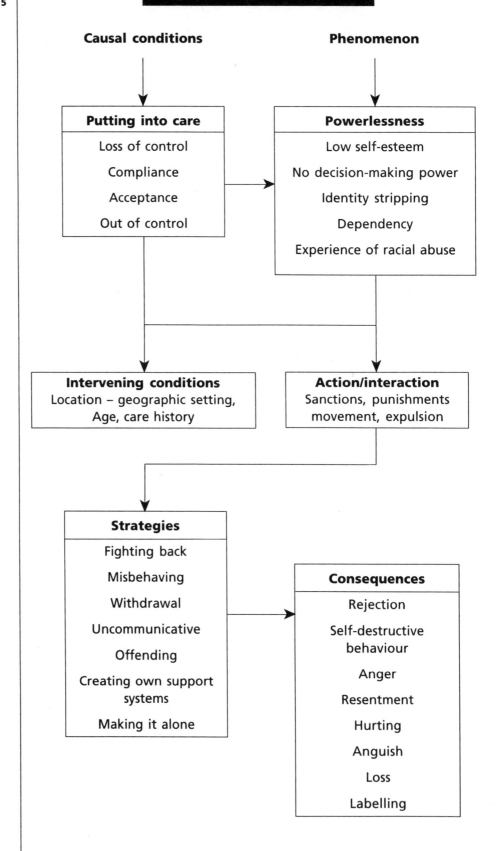

Biographic dimensions of the care trajectory

Causal conditions

Phenomenon

Putting into care

Loss of control

Compliance

Acceptance

Out of control

Powerlessness

Low self-esteem

No decision-making power

Identity stripping

Dependency

Experience of racial abuse

Intervening conditions
Location – geographic setting,
Age, care history

Action/interaction
Sanctions, punishments
movement, expulsion

Strategies

Fighting back

Misbehaving

Withdrawal

Uncommunicative

Offending

Creating own support
systems

Making it alone

Consequences

Rejection

Self-destructive
behaviour

Anger

Resentment

Hurting

Anguish

Loss

Labelling

The meaning of caring and non-caring and the conditions under which care was perceived as caring and non-caring

The analysis of the concepts of "caring" and "non-caring" are based on the respondents' words taken from the data. This is depicted in Figure 6 which shows the characteristics the young people attributed to the care experience. Their words show that they could not separate their negative and positive feelings about being in care, but there was more emphasis placed on the negative impact. This model illustrates how the two contradictory processes occur at the same time. The young people described care as "caring" when they found adults facilitating, helpful and supportive. It also applied to occasions when they were encouraged to give their further opinions or were included in the decision-making processes. For them, the important features of caring were the provision of love, security, consistency, stability, education and independence.

Adults who encouraged them were said to have made a positive difference to their care experience. As Figure 6 shows, this attribute was outweighed by non-caring qualities which could be divided into three categories. The first included feelings of powerlessness resulting from a lack of communication, excessive movement, institutionalisation, and feelings of abandonment and rejection. The second category included the effects of being a black person in a white care system which did not acknowledge their racial, cultural and identity needs. Over time this created feelings of isolation and stigmatisation, particularly for those in transracial placements in predominantly white neighbourhoods where they felt isolated. An absence of positive black role models left them with major questions about their own identity. Were they white? Were they black? These questions and feelings intensified as they grew older. Stigmatisation occurred on two levels: firstly from being in care and secondly from being black and having to endure and deal with racism and a general neglect of their physical care, such as skin and hair care, and dietary needs. The third category showed the marked lack of preparation for living independently of the care system.

Caring

Although all the young people saw a split between the caring and non-caring elements of being in care, the caring aspects were more pronounced in the testimonies of Mark and Marcel. While they acknowledged that being transracially placed dislocated them from their own racial and cultural group, the placements exposed them to good nurturing experiences. This perception greatly influenced their views about the importance of their ethnicity and culture. When there was evidence of non-caring, they tended to deny or minimise the negative and long-term impact on their lives. "Race" and culture were secondary to the care experience itself, which they felt was positive. When stability was achieved and positive attachments made, they both said this was an example of 'caring'.

> I have been loved and pushed. My foster parents didn't just want to see me leaving school without any qualifications and stuff. They pushed me, always trying to make me do my homework on time, to get good grades. I've never been in trouble with the police or anything, and they kept me on the straight path all the time. (Mark)

Here caring was associated by Mark with positive feelings towards the carers who he felt met his needs. These were the basic needs of love, security, understanding, encouragement and reassurance.

In Figure 7 I have used the work of Bryer[1] who developed a model to show people's

Figure 6

Connected themes of caring and non caring

Conditions or attributes of caring and non caring as determined by the young people

Caring

Non caring

Communicating
Helpful and supportive
Achieving
Keeping out of trouble
Having a free spirit
Being brought up
Financial security
Stable home
Being encouraged
Being there
Stability
Being independent

Controlling
Expulsion
Insecurity
Isolation
Alienation
Not a good place to be
Too much moving
No voice
No preparation
Being treated differently
Feeling powerless
Not being looked after
Neglecting physical needs
(hair & skin care)
Feeling self-conscious
Identity stripping
Racial abuse
Unsupporting
Stigmatising
No independence
Institutionalised
Not knowing anything

needs – basic needs which offer the boundaries within which people learn and grow. She described these as physical, educational, social, emotional and ethical. However, when planning for black children in care, "race" and culture should also be considered as basic needs. Figure 7 shows that the respondents had a multiplicity of needs including racial and cultural needs, which, if ignored, could create confusion. Discrepancies were evident in the respondents' attempts to reconcile what constituted adequate care. This was broadly based on their cognition of the emotional and physical aspects of care; what was absent was the development of racial and cultural identity.

> *I don't see myself as a black person and I don't see myself as a white person. Being black is my skin colour. I think there is a white culture and a black culture, but I don't know anything about the black culture. I suppose as a black person I'm very naïve.* (Marcel)

Caring was also associated with adults who had been perceived as helpful.

> *There was one man called Bob, I really liked him. He was really nice. Certainly not my social worker Brian. Joan got me all the fees for my education, but I hated the fact that she was forcing me to live with my mother, 'cause she never listened to anything I said.* (Marcel)

Emotional support was also valued as a sign of caring.

> *I had my first child taken off me, and there was this girl that came to the children's home and she would have a go. I would sit there with the tears welling up in my eyes, but I wouldn't let it out. Then the staff would tell the others, come on, gather round and I'd get the support from the other people. They made you talk and helped you with an aim for the following week. It was the experience alone that brought me out of my shell.* (Donneth)

Descriptive phrases were used to illustrate the supportive and caring elements that were possible within the care environment. These were crucial to problem solving, emotional support, self-preservation and assertiveness. Combined, these ingredients made the respondents' lives easier by making them more assertive and helping to develop survival skills.

> *It taught me that if you want anything it's there to be got, and you are entitled to it. Don't sit down and let others rush past and get it, stand up and get it yourself.* (Donneth)

Being befriended by social workers was greatly appreciated by many of the young people. It made them feel they were understood.

> *I remember a social worker called Jane and one called Robert. He was black. He was alright. Out of all the staff, they were the ones I'd have a conversation with. They put me on the right tracks, that I should have known already. It was them that showed me.* (Mark)

As Mark noted, black care staff played a crucial role, often offering support and guidance. They were the only black role models they had. Paula had direct experience of being protected by black workers against racism. Black workers also provided the young people with a positive image of "blackness" and the importance of taking a stand against racism.

Figure 7

Holistic approach to the needs of black children and young people

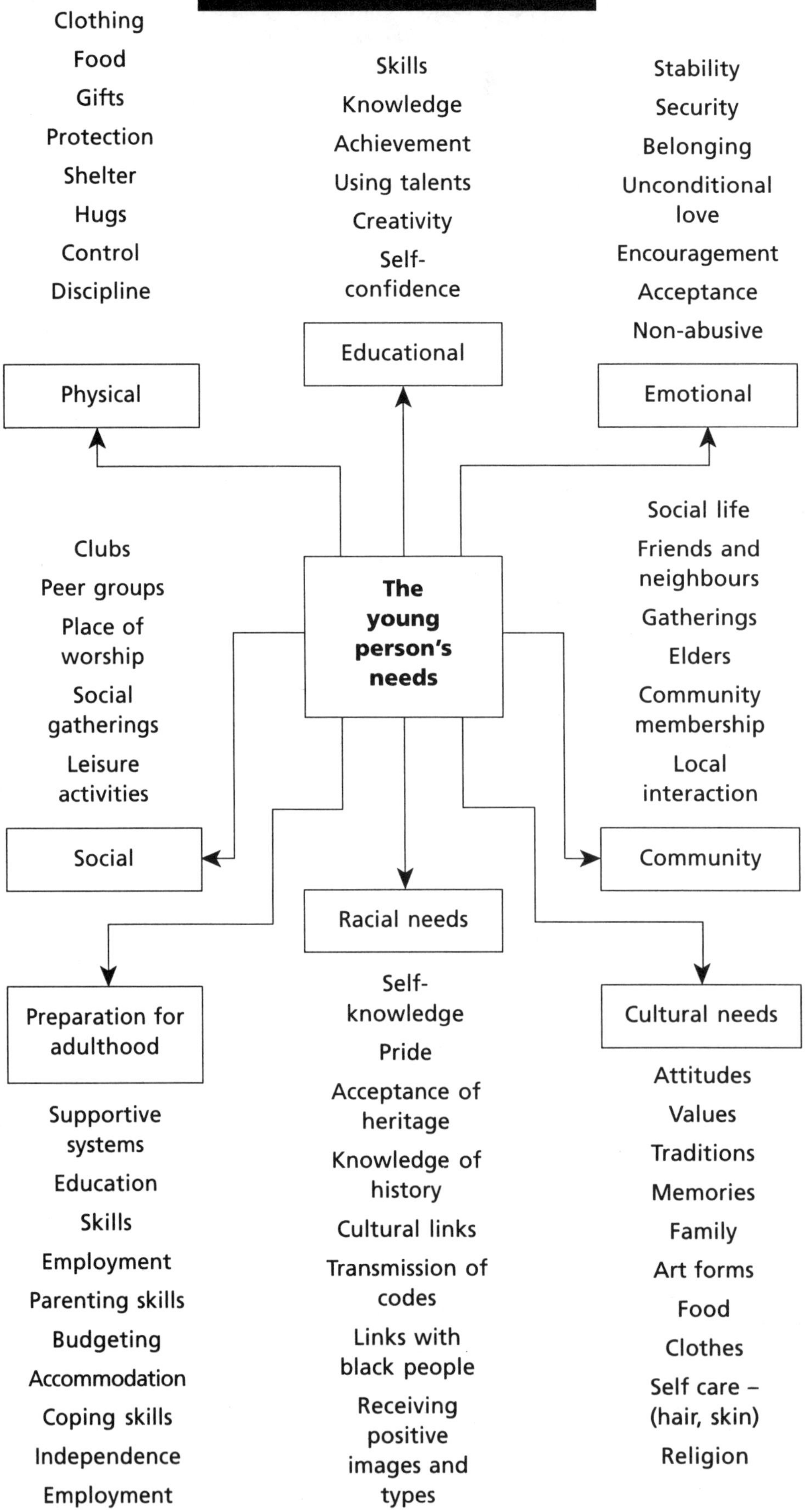

Physical

Clothing
Food
Gifts
Protection
Shelter
Hugs
Control
Discipline

Educational

Skills
Knowledge
Achievement
Using talents
Creativity
Self-confidence

Emotional

Stability
Security
Belonging
Unconditional love
Encouragement
Acceptance
Non-abusive

The young person's needs

Social

Clubs
Peer groups
Place of worship
Social gatherings
Leisure activities

Community

Social life
Friends and neighbours
Gatherings
Elders
Community membership
Local interaction

Racial needs

Preparation for adulthood

Supportive systems
Education
Skills
Employment
Parenting skills
Budgeting
Accommodation
Coping skills
Independence
Employment

Self-knowledge
Pride
Acceptance of heritage
Knowledge of history
Cultural links
Transmission of codes
Links with black people
Receiving positive images and types

Cultural needs

Attitudes
Values
Traditions
Memories
Family
Art forms
Food
Clothes
Self care – (hair, skin)
Religion

Having black staff helped a lot. The kids were really racist towards black staff and black kids. But there were a lot of black and Irish staff so racism was stamped. (Paula)

Being in care also provided some of the young people with material luxuries they never had previously. Many found themselves propelled from a poor background into a comfortable white middle-class family.

No-one seems to realise that although I've lost my biological mother I've gained five others. I've got my foster carers now who are terrific. I've got the people in Kent who I call mum and dad, and I've got my first foster parents who I still write to and hear from so I think I've gained. I'm really glad that I was fostered because it made me what I am and I wouldn't change any of it. (Marcel)

Effects on identity development

Racial identity was affected by the pattern of upbringing experienced by the young people (see Figure 8). Five of the respondents perceived themselves to be white while growing up in care. This led to confusion and separation from their racial and cultural heritage. It was a high price to pay for living in a white family and totally white environment.

There are about 11 coloured people, but the population is about 31,000. I've been brought up with white people so I've missed a lot of cultural things. When I see coloured children on the television in Ethiopia I feel something. But when I see coloured people in London and the way they act, I think some people have got an attitude problem. I think Oh, what the hell are they doing? I've got a whole lot of white views. (Mark)

Marcel felt that her life would have been 'amazingly different' if she had been cared for by a black family. Having been privately fostered with white families from the age of four, she showed a resistance to mixing with black people.

I wouldn't be doing what I am doing now. I know that, because I know how I live now, and how I lived when I was with my mother during the holidays. I would hate it. I would absolutely hate it. I wouldn't have a free spirit at all, I would just be scared all the time because I was scared of my mother all the time. (Marcel)

In Marcel's records, a social worker expressed concern about her lack of a positive black identity:

She has a poor sense of racial identity and cannot accept her African roots in a positive light. I feel she is ill prepared for the experiences she will have in the future and will be hurt by the amount of racism she will have to face in the future. (social worker)

The records also noted that Marcel was dismissive of her black culture and would not 'entertain the idea of a possible placement with a black family'. When I interviewed Marcel she behaved as if black families were disfunctional and lowly in status and power. To her, living with a white family gave her more opportunities.

I don't know what I'd be doing, probably working in Sainsbury's or

Figure 8

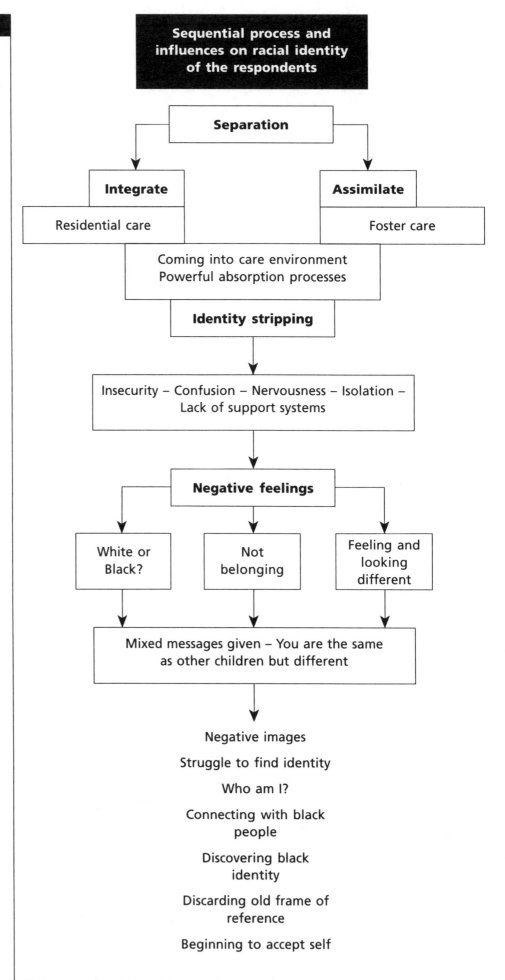

Sequential process and influences on racial identity of the respondents

Separation

Integrate
Residential care

Assimilate
Foster care

Coming into care environment
Powerful absorption processes

Identity stripping

Insecurity – Confusion – Nervousness – Isolation –
Lack of support systems

Negative feelings

White or
Black?

Not
belonging

Feeling and
looking
different

Mixed messages given – You are the same
as other children but different

Negative images

Struggle to find identity

Who am I?

Connecting with black
people

Discovering black
identity

Discarding old frame of
reference

Beginning to accept self

something, because I would have no motivation. (Marcel)

The young people had to balance many aspects of care with their perceptions of "race" and culture. Any sense of self was absorbed by the dominant culture. Being placed with a family took precedence over the racial and cultural needs of these young people. This included assimilating and internalising the views and attitudes of white carers.

> *My foster parents say there shouldn't be a distinction between colour.*
> *It's just that I've been brought up saying 'coloured'. They don't say*
> *'black' so they've kinda drummed it into me that people aren't black.*
> (Mark)

Strong views were also expressed about the nature of discrimination and its causes.

> *People say that when you go for a job and don't get it it's because you're*
> *black. But I think it may just be that you are not good enough for the*
> *job. I think that's just an excuse. Someone would have to come up to me*
> *and say 'you are a nigger' for me to realise it. People didn't say to me*
> *that black people are racist because they saw me as black so they*
> *wouldn't say that to me. I think that black people say that because they*
> *can't deal with the fact that they didn't get the job on their own merits.*
> (Marcel)

The failure to instil positive values about being black may not have been a conscious decision; carers were merely passing on their own values and attitudes. But as the young people in this case were black, the message they received caused confusion. Equally, the process of education and where they lived reinforced these values.

> *My foster parents don't say 'you're white', but it's the area. If there were*
> *more coloured people here, then I would be socialising with them. I*
> *reckon that I would have picked up some of the culture and for a start*
> *when I had a problem here with racism, I'd come and see my foster*
> *parents and they would say 'just leave it'. But I reckon if I had been*
> *with a coloured foster family they would have been able to explain it*
> *more and set my mind at rest. If I was in a black foster home, they*
> *would be able to relate to me more.* (Mark)

Secondly this reinforced the negative stereotypes of black people in general, hence the statement:

> *I've not been in trouble with the police.* (Mark)

Implicit in this statement was a belief that black children were more likely to get into trouble with the police. Add this to Mark's earlier statement that black people in London had an attitude problem, and it could be concluded that Mark made a noticeable distinction between himself and black people generally. Marcel added weight to this perception.

> *I'm trying to live down this image of all blacks as criminals and*
> *druggies.* (Marcel)

The young people were generally torn between wanting to be with black people but feeling it would be seen in a negative light such as 'having a chip on my shoulder'.

This pressure to take sides instilled a sense of self-hate and ridicule in them.

Sometimes, as I said, I would rather have been brought up with people who were black. Then again if I had, I would have grown up with a chip on my shoulder. (Tony)

Non-caring

The majority of the young people in this study, when assessing their care experience, placed a strong emphasis on the negative aspects of care, referred to here as "non-caring". There were several accounts of being treated differently, possibly because of their ethnicty.

In the foster home I went to, the way I got treated was like a charity case, so they could go out and say, 'Oh look, we've taken in a black child. What good people we are'. That's what I felt anyway. (Sandra)

These feelings led directly to searching questions:

Why am I in care? (Mark)
Why didn't my parents want me? (David)
Who am I? (Tony)

Professional ignorance and limited knowledge about how to handle the needs of black children also left their scars, particularly on the respondents' self-image and self-confidence. There was considerable anguish about skin care and hair care. Some had their hair cut off because the white carers could not cope with the texture. But this was done without any understanding of how damaging it was to the children.

I realised how naïve most of the white social workers were to my needs. Like taking me to white people to have my hair cut, and making them mess it up. (David)

Because they couldn't handle my hair or my sister's hair, they chopped it off short. Since then I've been very scared of hairdressers. I never knew how to look after my hair. I just used to go around with a big bush. (Cassie)

The actions of staff in residential homes were also described as non-caring. Sometimes the act in question directly related to ethnicity and was interpreted in different ways.

Like if a member of staff is against you and you don't click, they would make life hard for you. They always say we care, but you know they don't really. There was a lot of that. It does hurt, it's not very nice. (Denzil)

Discriminatory practices led to inequality in care.

You get stricter punishment than other people and things like that. Other people done the same things, but some people just treat you differently. (Denzil)

They would say we want to treat everyone equal, but we were not the same at the end of the day. I had to start caring for myself when I was young. They didn't care for me. (David)

Inequality was institutionalised not just in the care system but also in educational establishments. Without exception, all of the young people spoke of the racism they faced at school including name-calling by peers and discriminatory treatment by staff.

A lot of the staff used to pick on me like. I'll give you an instance. Say like if a white boy hit say another white boy, they just like sweep it under the carpet. But if it was me they'd call it assault and call in the police. I didn't really like it there. It wasn't a nice home. But I played it down. (Denzil)

He added:

It was very weird to me, especially the officer in charge. He was racist, definitely. Residential workers need training. (Denzil)

David recalled some of the remarks made to him.

I remember a lot of people have said things to me that I only understood when I was older. (David)

When asked what these were, he said:

For example, 'You must have just come off the banana boat'. People used to say to me AIDS come from Africa from foreigners. Racist remarks. (David)

The idea that being black contributed to a non-caring experience accentuated the young people's sense of being "different". While they had an awareness of "colour", they found it hard to express and discuss these feelings. Being in care did not help the young people understand why they were being treated differently as black people.

I didn't understand the difference between colour. I thought there was no difference. I thought they were my mother and father. I thought that I was white, but then as I grew older, I saw that I was definitely different and I became more conscious. (Natalie)

To Natalie the consciousness was bound up in the fact that:

Everyone tends to ask a lot of questions about why your child is black and you're white. You hear adults asking questions, and they know you can hear them. But they tend to ignore you as well 'cause they think that you don't understand. That's mostly my experience. (Natalie)

Being in care and being black was seen as a double jeopardy. The young people were labelled not only by the care system but by wider society. Finding employment was another obstacle to clear.

Being in care and being black doesn't help. When people ask about my school history and they see I have been sent all around the place I don't get the job. I once went for a job as a petrol attendant and I said I had been to [B] House. As soon as I said it I saw his face drop. (David)

The file records for David showed the extent to which care had been a stigmatising experience; he had also experienced considerable racism and felt rootless. David's need for a more integrated care approach was partially met when he elected to go to a home designated for black adolescents. However, his long history of being cared for by white people made him incapable of truly using the resource to his benefit.

> *Out of all the staff and all the homes I can remember, I saw two black staff. All the others were white people. All the boarding schools were pure white people except for [E] House. I was 14 years when I went there. It was run by Afro-Caribbean people with Afro-Caribbean food and everything. But I got kicked out as I was too bad.* (David)

Feelings of inferiority and being treated like second-class citizens were also reported.

> *People look down on you, think you are a troublemaker. It's just the way they react. If they find out anything they think you are a troublemaker. It's just the way they talk to you. Some people just look down on people in care.* (Paula)

> *Care is like having a criminal record.* (Cassie)

> *The only thing that bugs me is that people stereotype children who have been in care. Immediately they say you are bad, and that's not always true. That bugs me sometimes.* (Paula)

A lack of any will to solve problems was another concern identified by the young people. And there were very few signs that residential care staff took their "parental role" seriously.

> *If I had a problem no-one seemed to care whether the problem was solved or not.* (Cassie)

> *Care is a very bad influence. My solvent abuse and my shoplifting started from care. I had clashes with the staff. I mean physical clashes. But I think my worst experience was when I experimented with solvents.* (Donneth)

Feelings of being treated as a non-person and being talked down to were expressed. Social work jargon reinforced their sense of powerlessness and created a division between the professionals and the young people. This approach eroded their rights as children who needed to be heard.

> *Well, the social workers, I don't know if they learn it in college. They analyse everything you say. That's how they talk to you as if they think they are psychiatrists or something. People talk like that to you all the time.* (Sandra)

> *I think sometimes they get it muddled up because they say sometimes that children should always be with their parents. But it really screwed me and my sister up when we thought we were going to have to live with my real mum, and it didn't matter what we said. It took them ages and ages to understand we were telling the truth. They didn't listen to us at all from the beginning.* (Marcel)

In most cases, the term "care" did not fit or describe the experience of the sample. To survive, the young people adopted coping strategies such as submission to authority, self-denial, the internalisation of negative feelings, blaming parents, rebellion and physical violence.

Strategies for coping with non-caring

As a response to the findings I developed a concept called "making it alone". This was defined as a means of creating a power base that neutralised the sense of powerlessness. "Making it alone" caused the young people to develop other methods of self-protection to thwart the system or reverse the existing pattern of powerlessness. This was a concept derived from the conditions or attributes of non-caring (see Figure 6). This complex set of behaviours, which were not always positive, sometimes exposed them to even further danger, and increased their feelings of powerlessness. Despite the drawbacks, this strategy enabled the respondents to regain some control over their lives. It also helped them to address some of the conflicting and ambivalent feelings associated with being in care and, more specifically, being *black* and in care. "Making it alone" compensated for the lack of respect from certain adults such as residential staff and people in the community. It also made them feel that they could solve their own problems, the main ones being those listed below.

Feelings of isolation and being alone   This came as a result of where they lived. Transracial placements in all white communities gave little opportunity for the respondents to make contact with positive black role models. When some of them wanted an adult's help they were met with opposition, for instance, being told to ignore racist abuse or minimising its effects, ie. that it did not matter. When this happened the young person felt adults did not take their concerns about racial abuse seriously. Some suggested that often such abuse or incidents were played down.

Difficulties at school   The majority had little or no access to adult representation or advocacy. They were often subjected to unfair treatment bolstered by bullying and name-calling. Since they had no positive strategies to tackle the problems, they reacted either by submerging their feelings or being violent. A violent reaction made them a target for discrimination by teachers and the educational system. They experienced some of the most unethical, harsh controls and sanctions. Seven of the young people interviewed experienced permanent exclusion.

Getting into trouble with the police   Being denied access to education and being left without an aim or purpose, many quickly gravitated towards trouble and became a target for police attention. They were immediately identified not only because they were in care, but because of their colour, ie. being black. Becoming involved in delinquent behaviour became attractive to them, and before long they were committing crimes. This was compounded by feelings of rejection and a belief that no one really cared what happened to them.

Rejection by parents and the care system   Feelings of rejection were deep-rooted and haunted all the young people. They were perturbed by questions they could not answer such as: 'Why did my parents not want me?'; 'Why was I put into care?'; 'Why am I in a foster home?'; 'Why did she go with a coloured man?'; 'Why do people blame and stereotype children in care?'; 'Why was I moved all around the place?'; 'Why didn't they prepare me for leaving care?'.

Victim syndrome   Many felt stigmatised by the strong feelings that no one really cared about them, and therefore, they were alone. By the time they were ready to leave care the strategy of "making it alone" became a reality. With impoverished life skills and knowledge, they were literally left to rely on their own limited resources. Until leaving care, "making it alone" was an emotional response not necessarily calculated or thought about consciously by them.

What were the "making it alone" strategies?

I was forever lashing out . . . (Natalie)

We took a boy's money and mugged him. Basically we went round this guy's house and beat him up . . . (Denzil)

I did burglary, GBH, and unlawful wounding. I stabbed a man and beat him up . . . I was on drugs at the time . . . (David)

I ended up thumping people, I used to hit people . . . (Tony)

I bunked off school most of the time, because I didn't get into trouble for it. There was no-one there to care about you, so I just never went to school. I just went out all the time. (Sandra)

I started to rebel against staff, thinking they didn't care for me. (Cassie)

I fell pregnant on children's home premises. My mum went mad because as far as she was concerned if I was being cared for and supervised properly that wouldn't happen. The fact that I was 15 made it worse. (Donneth)

It must be said that the "making it alone" philosophy was not adopted by all the sample; a few managed to retain healthy relationships with members of their extended family and/or foster carers.

"Race" and culture in the care experience

For most of the young people in the sample the care experience did not reflect any positive images of "blackness". "Race" and culture form part of a world view – a frame of reference – within which to consider what is good, acceptable or desirable within that social sphere. For example, the young people who had denied their blackness saw the world from a white perspective. They needed to be accepted as white as a form of validation. Some of them were unaware of positive images of black people. Instead they emulated the attitudes and behaviour manifested in what they perceived to be the dominant culture.

All the young people pointed to their skin colour as the characteristic that singled them out for unequal and unfair treatment. In recalling memories relating to exclusion from the education system Donneth said:

I personally believe it had something to do with the colour of my skin.

Her feelings of unfair treatment and disadvantage were compounded by a feeling that she was more harshly punished than her white counterparts. For example, she was separated from her peers, allocated a home tutor and sent to an annex for children with learning difficulties, for children far less capable than herself.

I was disruptive at my middle school when I got put into care. The school refused to take me on. I was excluded. I was suspended for little things. I got excluded for something I shouldn't have been excluded for. I went to school in a blouse. The only thing that was different was that I had blue stripes and the other girl had red stripes. I was summoned to the deputy head's office and she wasn't. I was excluded and she wasn't. (Donneth)

Name-calling and taunting were common forms of racial abuse reported by all the young people.

Nobody ever said anything to me about my colour. Only at primary school where racism was really bad. (Denzil)

When I first came across racism I was at junior school. I didn't know what it meant. I would just leave it, but I was hurt. But why am I different from other people? I used to blame it on my mum. In a way I used to say why did she go with a coloured guy? The main thing is I was really hurt at the time. But when you get older you have to deal with it. (Mark)

I remember when I was at junior school and I used to be called 'black Jack'. I remember one of my friends called me a black bitch and that just absolutely hit me. I cried for days and days. (Marcel)

When I was in [H] House the only black people you would see was those from the home, and I got called racist remarks from white people. The children were also a bit prejudiced. If a white person was talking to me they would be called a nigger lover and I would be called a black bitch. I got into trouble at school for that, cause a boy called me a nigger and I went for him. (Cassie)

I do feel now that I am a black person. I have arguments with my darker-coloured skinned friends. As I see it, if I was walking the streets, they'd shout 'nigger' not 'half-caste'. If people say 'Where are you from?', I say 'London' and they say 'No, originally where are you from?'. I'd say 'London' and they'd say 'Your grandparents'. They trace it back until it's outside England. (David)

Staff also appeared to be racist. Not only was there a failure to recognise racism and deal with it, in some cases it was perpetrated by staff. Their own misunderstandings and misapprehensions about the "blackness" of those in their care often led to more severe punishments. It was the mistreatment by staff that characterised the young people's experiences in care; for many, it was their most harrowing experience.

When you're like a black kid you notice that you get a lot of attention in the class. It's like the teachers just kicking you out, like trying to make a point of you to other kids. (Tony)

I got a lot of racism at the community home. A lot of staff used to pick on me. (Denzil)

I had it drummed into me that people aren't black. (Mark)

Discrimination meant that:

You get stricter punishments than other people, and things like that.

Other people done the same things, but some people just treat you differently. (Denzil)

Some of the young people had to develop a number of strategies to protect themselves.

Fighting back

After an incident of racial abuse, Donneth was outraged at the inherent injustice and inequality and interpreted this behaviour as 'wrong'.

I just went and beat up a boy and got told to leave him alone and I swore at the dinner lady. She refused to come back to school until I wrote an apology. She refused to come back to work, until I wrote an apology to her, even though I explained what had happened. That was wrong, cause they should punish the boy because he shouldn't have said what he said. (Donneth)

Physical violence or 'lashing out' was used as a common method of retaliation. At the time, it seemed the only way to express their anger.

Not thinking about it

Another approach was to ignore what was happening, particularly the personal hurt and pain caused by racism.

I ignored it. I like the colour of my skin. I don't care, I don't care what people say. I think my sister is more unsure of it. When she used to come to me I told her to ignore it. But she can't because it hurts. (David)

I didn't tell anybody, only my mum and she would just say 'Ignore it'. (Mark)

I used to ignore a lot of it [racism]. It didn't bother me because, at the end of the day, this is a mixed society. I just ignored them and I didn't let it bother me. I had better things to think about. (Paula)

Internalising it

I was scared of black people to be honest. (Cassie)

I know there are white people who are supposed to be racist against black people. A lot of my close friends, my boyfriend and whatever, are white, because you are brought up with that. You think they can't be racist. (Marcel)

I was white as far as I was concerned. The only thing is my skin colour wasn't white, it was brown. (Cassie)

Minimising it

I just think it doesn't matter. (Mark)

People say there is a culture, and I would like to think there isn't. You're just an individual. (Marcel)

But they are just jealous because they have got to go out in the sun to get a nice colour on their skin, while I got mine. (Cassie)

That's it, I don't see myself as a black person and I don't see myself as a white person. (Marcel)

Absorbing it

If my foster parents had said, 'You are black', where would I be now? (Marcel)

I used to look down on black people and that, and be really really racist and say racist things. (Sandra)

I ended up being racist against black people, 'cause I used to live with white foster people, and I think they were racist. They always used to look down on black people and think they lived in huts. I use to think they lived in huts like in the Tarzan films. (Sandra)

Living with white people put my views one way, like sort of towards white. (Mark)

Defence systems

The various strategies outlined above can be interpreted as defence systems which helped the young people to cope with the stress and anxieties created by racism. These reactions were knee-jerk reactions and were linked to self-preservation in the absence of dependable adults. They became a way of dealing with anxiety, fear, isolation and the sense of non-caring. Though initially negative, and at times fraught with danger, these commonly experienced defence systems helped them to survive. But it has to be said that the long-term emotional damage to seven of the respondents – Cassie, David, Tony, Marcel, Mark, Natalie and Sandra – was immeasurable.

Breakthrough stage

The important stage of breakthrough could not be reached without the positive and enlightened help of others. The following accounts show how this process occurred and the people who helped.

When I was at senior school, there was this black guy called Jim. He like sort of took me under his wing. (Mark)

My advantage as a black person was that I had my family before going into care. So I knew about the way black people lived their lives. (Donneth)

Evidence shows that when there were black members of staff in residential units, the young people felt more supported and less isolated.

My social worker was black, and when I wanted to talk to somebody she was there, she was always there. She helped me through all the emotional patches when my child was taken into care. (Donneth)

My key worker, I would go and see her, she was black. The fact that I had a black key worker helped. Having black staff helped a lot. The kids were really racist towards black staff and black kids. The staff never had the time to sit down and deal with those kids. They were too unruly. (Paula)

I'm not being funny or anything, but I think that black people are better off with their own families. (Tony)

Race and culture are very important to me. I can't explain how, but it's like a feeling . . . You know the feeling and stuff, how you feel about yourself. (Natalie)

There was a couple of people who did really care. One of them was a black lady. I still see her now. (Sandra)

When my friend came into care – that was when I learned about black culture. Otherwise I would know nothing. I couldn't remember seeing one black member of staff. (Cassie)

Commentary

When the young people were confronted by racism they used the "making it alone" strategy. The lack of supportive systems and networks led to the introduction of a second model of "making it alone" which was overlaid with the theme of "race". In this second model, a more positive and proactive stance was assumed by the young people who turned to black staff, relatives, peers, friends, black foster carers and the black community. The principal reason for this was to reinforce their own sense of identity and mobilise different forms of mental and emotional support. The reason for "making it alone" stemmed from the realisation that those charged with their care for an extensive period made no attempts to facilitate meaningful contact with black people with whom the young people could identify. These black people had the resources to prepare them for life in a multiracial and multicultural society. For the respondents, contact with black people had been largely discouraged, withheld by white foster carers and social workers.

Significantly, the young people did not receive any permission from caretakers to make these connections until faced with leaving care. Their time in care had lulled them into a false sense of security. In this context, "making it alone" was used as a protective mechanism to insulate them against the harsh realities of racism. "Making it alone" was also intrinsically related to care placements and the type of people who were carers.

Transracial placements

Within the context of this research, transracial placements refer to the placement of black children in white foster/or adoptive families or in all-white residential homes. All of the study sample had, at some time, experienced this type of care. All except Mark and Marcel had an experience of residential care.

David had a brief period in a residential establishment staffed by black people, but it was of very short duration and had no impact on his well-being. The timing of this placement was far too late to make any significant difference to the quality of this life-long care experience. He admitted that by the time this help came it was too late. In his words: 'I was too bad'. One of the consequences of transracial placement is the isolation that results.

When I was in Devon, there were a lot of white people and me. How can they understand, when the white kids said 'Look, a nigger'. They couldn't understand. They did nothing. (David)

This study shows evidence that such placements exposed most of the young people, as children, to overt and covert forms of racism and discrimination. In the absence of protective mechanisms and supportive frameworks they were unable to develop positive coping skills. This had a significant bearing on the "making it alone" concept. White family life was presented as a better and more protective environment but it fell far short of this ideal. The majority of the young people's carers had neglected to take appropriate action to safeguard and protect them from various forms of oppression. The strategies they were offered, for example, to "ignore" it, did nothing to ease the pain they felt.

The data gathered showed active forms of racism – incidents of verbal racial abuse such as name-calling, taunting and freezing out. Physical and emotional abuse were also common occurrences. Racism was also experienced in the school setting. Placements had an impact on how the young people fared in the education system. Support systems were clearly lacking. Lack of achievement was almost certainly connected to their status as children in care. Although four (only one male) had some educational qualifications, the majority were affected emotionally and intellectually. This finding reinforces those of a number of studies conducted since the 1970s that show a strong correlation between the underachievement of black children in British schools and the prevalence of racism within the education system. The way carers and professionals responded to these problems was significant. The young people felt that adults did not encourage them to express their feelings about what was happening. On the contrary, they were told to repress these feelings. In finding their own solutions and reacting in negative, sometimes aggressive ways, they found themselves, and not the perpetrators, punished and blamed.

Figure 9 breaks down the impact of care on racial identity. The family is referred to as A, the care system as B, the role of "race" and culture in the care experience as C and the black community as D. The period when the young people were taken into care was when there was a continuing immigration of black families from the Caribbean and Africa. Vital support systems such as the extended family and friends were lost. There was little awareness of community services, and the response to the needs of newly arrived families by social services departments was very poor. When these families had difficulties, their children were vulnerable. Some factors which heightened their vulnerability included:
• living in poor and impoverished conditions;
• limited support and preventive systems and services, such as day nurseries;
• loss of extended family and friends who could help in times of need;
• racial discrimination; and
• a tendency by professionals to view black families in need pejoratively.

When the young people in A (black family) were deemed to be in need of alternative care, they were moved to B (care system). In area B, very little was known about the black child. The "colour-blind" Eurocentric model of care was applied which treated all children as the same. There was very little in common between the young black children and their carers who were largely white. Once in area B, the majority were cut off from A and D. The "colour-blind" approach meant that C was overlooked.

Identity stripping

For young black children, identity stripping occurs when identity is diluted through neglect, "colour-blindness" and racism. Separation from other black people sustains the process. In this study it seemed that children were usually stripped of their culture in different ways, for example, the absence of black adults

Figure 9

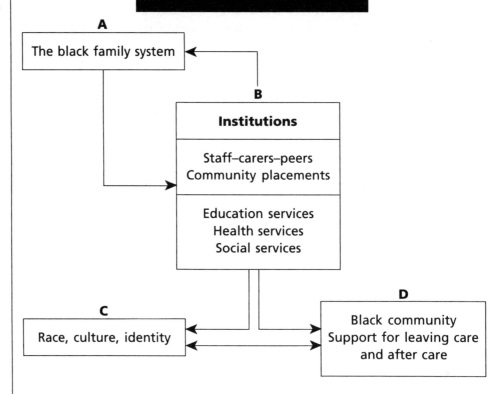

Model of care and its impact on racial identity of the respondents

A
The black family system

B
Institutions

Staff–carers–peers
Community placements

Education services
Health services
Social services

C
Race, culture, identity

D
Black community
Support for leaving care
and after care

This diagram shows the links that have to be made between black families, the care system and the black community to encourage positive feelings in young people about their race, culture and black identity.

who could be role models, the unavailability of ethnic foods, the lack of literature, books or posters with multicultural themes, and the lack of opportunities to learn about black history.

One young person said that making contact with black children at school made her feel conscious and different. She felt superior to them, and at times felt excluded by them because of her perception of herself. With no exposure to any black influences, the young people based their views on what they had seen and heard in the media and from carers. This led to so-called "white views" which held negative perceptions of blackness.

I didn't have a very good deal. I didn't learn about my own culture or anything because I was with a white foster family for the majority of my life and the people in the residential homes were mostly white. I didn't learn anything. (Sandra)

The consequence was the development of racial prejudice among the young people themselves.

I ended up being racist against black people, 'cause I used to live with white foster people and I think they were racist. (Sandra)

There was a great deal of confusion about what culture meant.

I haven't got a culture myself. If there is a culture, it's white. (Mark)

For me being black is my skin colour, because I think there is a white culture. But I don't know anything about the black culture. (Marcel)

Culture was defined as the way people live their lives, the food they eat, the music they listen to, and their historical background. Adopting white values meant that vital lessons about culture were never discovered.

I ought to know more about my culture. I don't even know how to cook West Indian food, and it's annoying. I like it, but I can't cook it. I watch my friends do it, but I can't do it. They have been taught from a very young age. Girls know how to cook and fix their hair. I don't know any of that. It would have been nice if I was put with a black family. I would know more about my culture. (Cassie)

Culture was also described as a valuable asset, one that could not be truly imparted by white people.

Black culture is where a child will grow up to know West Indian food . . . they have to learn about the way we cook, learn about music and jazz, they all come from black people. English people do not know how to bring this out in the black child. They do not know anything about our hair, all they know is that we've got tighter hair than they do. As far as I'm concerned that isn't enough to bring up a child. (Donneth)

The younger they were when transracially placed the more vulnerable the young people were to identity stripping. As caretakers strived to treat them the same as everyone else, culture was dismissed as unimportant.

Before leaving care, you've got to know your race and your culture. I think that people can say that you're this and you're that, but it's a learning process, not a regimented thing. You learn from your own experiences. So if you've had racist trouble you learn from that. (Mark)

A lot of my white friends say 'I don't see you as black really'. (Marcel)

The absence of a cultural benchmark for some of the young people led to a lack of racial boundaries. For example, Marcel sometimes found herself making racist jokes because 'they were funny'.

Natalie's file records noted how her foster carers had showed little interest in her colour or culture. They treated her as if she were a white child. A report was written by a black social worker who had been co-opted to the case to give advice. She expressed concern about a number of areas. Health care, skin care, and the child's emotional need for contact with relatives and with positive black role models were among them – Natalie's request for contact with her family was blocked by the foster family. It was reported that the foster family's reaction to the black social worker was dismissive. A recommendation for Natalie's needs to be reviewed and for the appropriateness of the placement to be considered was made. Nevertheless, the placement continued and disrupted several years later. At this time a white social worker wrote:

I think this child enjoys the blackness of being with her relations, which is something she had to forget in her foster family. (social worker)

Natalie was consumed by her loss of racial and cultural identity. Long-term alienation increased her desire to find her "roots". Natalie recognised the inherent tendency to 'go with races other than black'. This was a constant source of internal conflict and tension, which was exacerbated by incidents such as going on holiday with her foster parents when the white children refused to get into the swimming pool while Natalie was in it.

It is things like that that stick in my mind, and it's like I was always with my foster parents, I had no-one my own age to go with. Do you see what I mean? (Natalie)

She went on to say that "race" and culture were important to her, but she found it hard to verbalise what they meant:

I can't exactly explain how, it's like a feeling.

But Natalie knew it was a concept that 'care doesn't show you'.

No-one sits down and tells you 'Look, this is where you come from and this is what happens'. No-one sits down with you at all. (Natalie)

During this stage there was a breakthrough which led to the process of "identity unfolding". This was usually triggered by making contact with another black person. This was apparent in the study. The following examples show how significant this was.

When I was in the residential home a black woman helped me out, you know, talked to me and that. (Cassie)

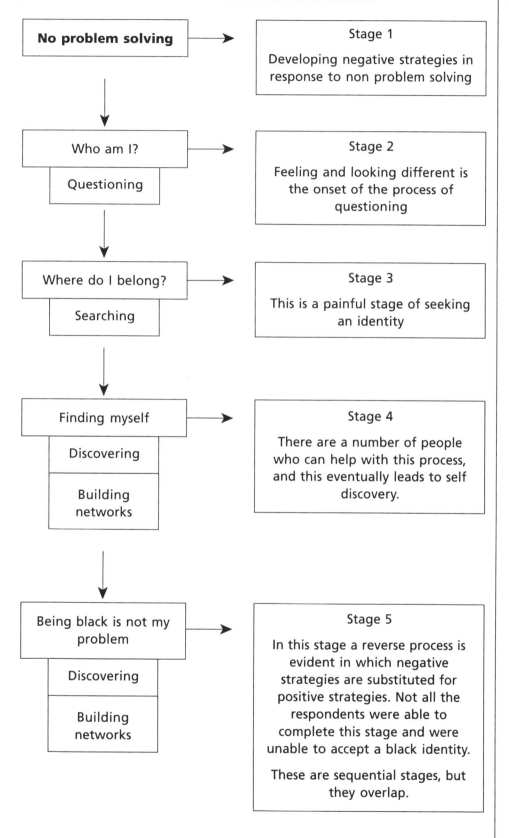

The five stages of making it alone

No problem solving →

Stage 1

Developing negative strategies in response to non problem solving

Who am I?

Questioning

→

Stage 2

Feeling and looking different is the onset of the process of questioning

Where do I belong?

Searching

→

Stage 3

This is a painful stage of seeking an identity

Finding myself

Discovering

Building networks

→

Stage 4

There are a number of people who can help with this process, and this eventually leads to self discovery.

Being black is not my problem

Discovering

Building networks

→

Stage 5

In this stage a reverse process is evident in which negative strategies are substituted for positive strategies. Not all the respondents were able to complete this stage and were unable to accept a black identity.

These are sequential stages, but they overlap.

Figure 10

Such contacts were often initiated by the young person in search of lost roots.

I would say, go and find out more. To me it's very important 'cause it's about being a black person. I now see my family regularly several times a week which I never really had before. The first time I saw my mother, I could only see her once a week and that was because of the Care Order and the social worker. And then it was allowed that I could stay there weekends, and then I wanted to see her more and more, and I wanted to be with my family. (Natalie)

In the cases of Mark, Marcel and Tony whose racial identities did not unfold, they opted for a "white" way of life.

Figure 10 shows that most of the young people were separated from their family by coming into care. Once in care – residential or foster care – they faced pressure to assimilate and integrate. The presence of racism (institutional and personal) within the care system restricted the development of a positive black identity. As a result, many young people's needs – racial and cultural – remained unmet, creating a sense of powerlessness.

In the third section of Figure 10, the findings indicated that inevitably there was a struggle to find identity. Later, and during the pubescent years, there was a struggle to find a black identity. Reunification with relatives can trigger this process. However, for a black identity to unfold there had to be a disassociation and separation from the negative model followed by a commitment to a positive black identity. For this to happen, it was necessary to embark on a journey of self-discovery. This involved, for example, making connections with other black people. The one way identity could unfold was by discarding the negative aspects of white identity and retaining the positive, particularly for those of mixed heritage.

Preparation for leaving care

Most of the young people in the study had not been adequately prepared for leaving care. As with all children in care, preparation needs to be made for finding accommodation, employment, managing finances and being equipped with practical life skills for the transition to adulthood. For the respondents in this study, lack of after care support was a common theme, as was poor information on the duties and responsibilities of the social services department once they were discharged from care. Making contact with their birth families became important for the young people. But for the transition from care to be successful, their has to be appropriate planning and financial support.

I was straight out and into my dad's accommodation and that was it. I mean I turned 16 and I had to leave the home. (Cassie)

Attempts to restructure broken and dislocated family relationships became part of the transition process. The supportive role families can provide during the process of leaving care cannot be under-estimated. It is up to local authorities to ensure that the young people are not hindered during this period of upheaval and turmoil.

I wish social services could give everyone, not just black people, a helping hand, because when you feel sheltered, you feel so wrapped up in cotton wool. And then all of a sudden you have to go out and you have to fend for yourself. I just really wish they could sit down and teach them. (Natalie)

This statement shows why effective communication about the pros and cons of leaving care needs to take place way in advance of the actual event. With one exception, the young people in this study did not receive preparation for leaving care. What was evident from the data was the lack of personal preparation to meet the challenges of life, particularly for those in residential care who felt institutionalised. Those who had been in foster care were less anxious because they felt able to appropriately remain in the placement, or to return at a later stage; in other words, just like you would do in any family. Two young people (Mark and Marcel) who were hoping to go on to university tended to play down the importance of preparation for leaving care. They did not want to feel any differently from other children leaving "ordinary" homes. They felt that their care experience had been successful. Yet it is important to note that they found it difficult to accept a black identity. They seemed sure that they would have a home with their white carers.

I know what it's like not to have money, so I know how to balance it out. Because I'm going to drama school, you don't have time to think about things like that. I will be living with other people. (Marcel)

Despite strong links with foster carers, some of the respondents did not receive any preparation or advice from them on leaving care. It was taken for granted by the social services departments that this would be offered by the foster carers. However, there were no indications of where they would eventually settle and what their long-term future would be. Thus there was a tendency to further delay achieving independence.

My foster parents said I could stay here with them. My ambition has been to go away to university. So I haven't really thought about moving out or getting a job or anything. I have been accepted at Leeds University, so I'll go in September. If I go there I'll come back here. That's why I count this as my home. (Mark)

If I leave care, I'll still be living here won't I? So it won't really change. (Tony)

Remaining in the black extended family also had a significant and positive impact on leaving care and skills development.

My race and culture is very important to me. I was always learning about my roots. I learned about people like Martin Luther King and black history. I've always been that way. (Paula)

Half of the young people in the study had strong family support from foster carers for leaving care. For all the others this was an awesome, even fearful, rite of passage. On a conscious level, they were now faced with the prospect of "making it alone". They were acutely aware of their limitations, immaturity, low self-confidence and limited practical life skills, and the inadequate guidance they had received. Graphic language was used to describe this experience.

I thought I would die, it was really scary. I remember having dreams; I was so scared. I just didn't know. The biggest fear was being alone. (Natalie)

When I left care, I thought 'How would I get a place of my own? How do I go about supporting myself? Where do I get food to live on?' The big worries are the tasks and how to cope with the loneliness. (Sandra)

I wasn't taught how to live my life. I had to come out of care the hard way, and it's very hard, very, very hard. (Cassie)

I don't think that the social worker that I had at the time knew that in the accommodation I went into straight after the children's home I was nearly raped by the landlord. I don't even think she knows that. I never had no contact with no social worker from the time I left the children's home until a month before my second child was born. Because of my previous experience, they put her on the Child Protection Register, and then I had contact again with a social worker. (Donneth)

Although there was a longing to leave institutional care, there were equally deep fears about the future. Leaving care at 16 or even 18 is not synonymous with maturity. These are not ages when young people automatically assume the responsibilities that go hand in hand with being an adult. Rather, this is a time of great anxiety and trepidation.

I was not prepared for what I'm going through now. I thought when you come out of care it was going to be easy. But it hasn't been. It's been one problem after the other. (Cassie)

There was no preparation. (Natalie)

I was prepared for nothing, nothing at all. (Donneth)

Teaching and learning were described as the key elements missing in the care process.

I wasn't really taught. I fell pregnant at 18. I realised I had to start settling down. When I first left care, I didn't have any money. I was on the Youth Training Scheme at £26.00 per week. I had to give my dad money for food and electricity, buy my own food, toiletries, clothes and so on. My bedroom wasn't even carpeted. I just had a bed that was given to me by the children's home. That was it. (Cassie)

Dealing with racism in the wider society should also be part of the preparation for young black people leaving care.

Britain is a very racist country, I have to say that. Racism is a very hard thing to cope with. If you are not white it's harder, and I think that while a child is in care they should be taught about racism. (Cassie)

Sometimes when you see people on the tube, they look at you sort of strange. I always stare back at them. But it's little things as well that make me more aware of being black now. (Marcel)

If a child is in care from young, they should sit down and talk to them about their race and culture. (Paula)

The first three-bedroomed accommodation I got, the next door neighbour was anti-black, didn't like black people. The third day after I moved in she called the police to say I was stealing milk. I had the Drug Squad watching my house because she went and reported that drugs were being sold from my premises. She assaulted us with water. (Donneth)

When asked how they could have been prepared, the young people had difficulty understanding what the term preparation actually meant.

> *It wasn't until the later stages that I realised I wasn't a child no more. I was classed as a young person and it wasn't until I realised that, that I started to use the care system to my benefit. While I was under their establishment, on their premises I was fine. It was when I left that my problems began.* (Donneth)

> *I didn't even know that my name could go on a housing list, and that I had to get points. I only found that out last year. Social workers should always ask the child about their feelings. 'How do you feel? Are we doing enough for you? What would you like us to do?'* (Natalie)

> *If a child is coming out of care, I think that they should be taught how to cope in the outside world. I had troubles since the day she [pointing to her daughter] was born. I've had more trouble with this flat, and I don't know how to cope. I'm in debt. I have problems paying my bills. If I can't pay the bills in seven days, I don't know how to look after my money and sort out money for the bills, and rent and food and so on, 'cause I was never taught how to. When you come out of care you should at least be taught how to live.* (Cassie)

> *I have left the children's home now, but the Care Order does not end until October 1993. I live here alone in this flat. I found it for myself and the social worker came and had a look to make sure it was alright.* (Paula)

> *They just got me a flat and said 'Off you go', that was it.* (Sandra)

After leaving care there were no available or accessible safety nets or support networks. Most of the young people were left to make it alone with the onus of responsibility resting firmly on them. Living skills had to be developed quickly to enable survival to take place.

> *I did a lot of scrimping, saving, screaming, shouting, stamping of feet and demanding to get what I wanted. Since I've left care I've had loads of addresses. I've moved from here, to there, to there, to there. The only way I managed to get permanent accommodation was when I had my little girl.* (Donneth)

The lack of domestic skills mostly affected the females, but by and large all the young people suffered from a lack of basic preparation. Some of the young women expressed disappointment that they were not taught parenting skills to help them become mothers. The young men were concerned about accommodation and job opportunities. They were left to discover through trial and error the importance of budgeting, shopping and paying bills. Managing money was one of the major challenges.

> *I've only just in the last two years sat down with a pen and pad to work my money out. If I was shown how to do that before, maybe I wouldn't be in such financial problems as I am now.* (Donneth)

> *There was money problems, that was the main one. I didn't get the help I needed, or the support I needed.* (Cassie)

Leaving care was difficult for Natalie, particularly as she disrupted her long-term foster placement to search for her cultural roots.

> *I wanted to move, and I asked my boyfriend's parents about being black. She said she would like me as her daughter. So we went to social services about me moving in with them and they said yes. Basically, it was a roof over my head. But after saying yes, they then said no. Then, they kept changing their minds. Then she asked about other accommodation and all they would offer me was bed and breakfast accommodation which is something I've seen before and I would not like to go through that. They said 'Get a job and work to get a flat', that's basically what I was told. In other words, 'You are in the big wide world now and you have to fend for yourself like other people'. I am still very scared of the big wide world.* (Natalie)

Independence was often delayed as some of the young people had to turn to social services for financial assistance. Sandra's file records showed how often she was bailed out by the department. This was equally true in David's case whose long experience in residential care left him institutionalised and incapable of living in the community. Asked what kind of problems were most prominent, he said:

> *The main thing was boredom really. In a children's home you are surrounded by any amount of people. Then you are on your own. I coped, but mind you I'm like a survivor. I've coped with a lot of things that most people wouldn't cope with.* (David)

The fact that this interview took place in prison showed that David was a long way from coping and that his survival depended on institutional living. It is questionable whether he will ever be able to live independently in the community.

Two young people had been given financial assistance with education fees: one had been helped with accommodation costs and had to fight to have the amount increased and another found her own accommodation and received help from social services to top up her benefits. Two went into supported lodgings, one was left to live in unfavourable conditions, and one said he received no financial help at all. One was placed with her father at 16 with minimal support, and one received no preparation and was immediately placed in bed and breakfast accommodation.

> *I would have expected them to give me something in my pocket but I got nothing.* (Denzil)

> *Young people get different amounts of money. No-one has told me what my rights are.* (Sandra)

> *I don't really know. I'm not sure what's actually happening. Social services have paid all my fees for drama school and travelling expenses this year, but then when I leave, I don't know what will happen and whether all the money will stop or if I will get more. I don't know. No-one has come to talk to me to say you're leaving care on this day and this is happening.* (Marcel)

When asked how they thought black young people should be prepared for leaving care, none of them had any clear ideas. They did not perceive their needs to be different from any other young person leaving care. 'I haven't got a clue' or 'I don't know', were common responses.

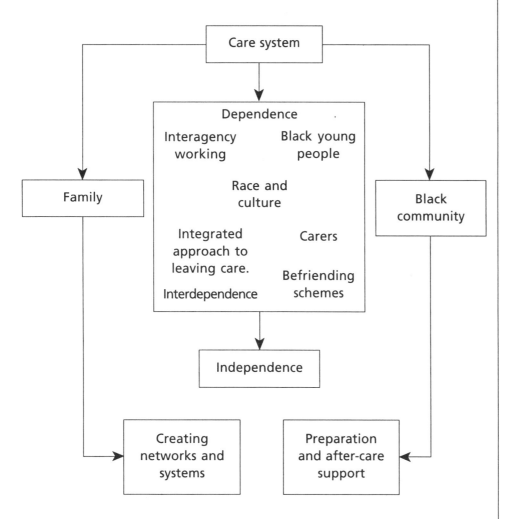

Figure 11

This diagram shows the type and nature of work that is required to achieve an integrated approach to leaving care. A process that begins with dependence on state care should become less significant. Planning and integration are integral to the process of preparation. This will eventually lead to independence and a programme of support systems through to aftercare. There is a need to diminish the boundaries between the care systems and all those involved in the planning process. Race and culture are integral to the process of preparation for leaving care. This should be included as a discrete category in all planning and review systems for leaving care and transition to independence.

I suppose there are a lot of black people in general, kids on the streets, ain't it, just come out of care and that, and they haven't been put up right. They should look out for those people really. I've got a home here. (Denzil)

For half the young people, leaving long-term local authority care was one of the most difficult and testing experiences they had had to face. Without dialogue with their caregiver about the nature of the task before them, they felt totally alone. This is why the experience of leaving care was described as 'frightening', 'scary', 'lonely' and 'frustrating'. For these feelings to be tackled, a high level of planning and interdisciplinary liaison are necessary; this is illustrated in Figure 11. It shows that the move from dependence should be augmented by interdependence during and after care, leading to independence and appropriate separation from the care system.

Reference

1 Bryer M, *Planning in Child Care*, BAAF, 1988.

Departmental policies

Two senior workers from the two local authorities participating in this study were interviewed. In Social Services Department A, there were no specific policies relating to the care of black children. The prevailing view was that it was better to place a black child in a white family than to allow the child to remain in residential care, and that the welfare of the child and planning for the child had priority over a "same-race" placement policy. There was also a lack of policy directives to reinforce the importance of black children's needs for a positive and healthy identity development.

In commenting on "same-race" placements, it appeared that although such placements should apply as a principle, planning was the most important element: 'It may be more appropriate to have alternative non "same-race" placements which would actually give them more security.' It was felt that these were 'complex issues' and so no hard and fast rules could apply, and each individual case would be considered on its merits. This suggested that there were no guidelines for managers and staff who were left to make their own decisions based on value judgements rather than what was in the best interests of the black child. The statutory child care review system, they believed, would act as a monitoring mechanism.

In both Departments A and B, institutional and personal racism were highlighted by the participants as major stumbling blocks to reform.

The major areas of concern were:
- lack of recruitment of black staff;
- lack of recruitment of black foster carers and adoptive parents;
- lack of appropriate training programmes;
- no policy statement and guidance for staff on "same-race" placements; and
- no policy statement and code of practice on racism relating to children in care.

Despite the existence of equal opportunities policies, few black staff and black carers were recruited. At the time of this research, there were only two black people in management positions in Department A. Ethnic record keeping was its most detailed policy, but this was not monitored and whether or not staff completed this question on their referral form was optional. This made it difficult to produce statistical evidence.

Likewise, there were no specific policies formulated on leaving care, even though there was a recognition that young black people were more vulnerable than their white counterparts at the hands of the criminal justice system – Department A was aware that black youths within the care system were more likely to receive custodial sentences. There was a high report rate of racial attacks on young black people in residential institutions within this department. A large number of young black people were also experiencing placement breakdown after being rejected by white carers. Those leaving care had restricted access to fostering services for teenagers (teencare) and supported lodgings. Racism in residential care was known to be pervasive, but there were no specific strategies to deal appropriately with this problem.

Department B did not have a policy on "same-race" placements. It advocated a more general framework for all children in care with a policy on "race matching". This meant that the department had a policy of placing black children in transracial placements, particularly for short-term placements. There was also a policy not to place children under 12 years in residential establishments. This was a significant change given that most of the young people from this department had been placed in residential care for several years. There was little communication on the precise needs of black children. It was assumed that children from "West Indian" families could fit in more easily with British traditions than, say, Asian children who were seen as having distinctive languages and religions. Children with one white and one black parent were automatically placed with white carers. The policy's weakness was that it led to a misassessment of need.

There was limited recruitment of black carers for fear that they would not be used. There was no policy of placing white children with black carers. When black carers were recruited it was specifically for black children. As a result, black long-term carers were underused, leading managers to scrutinise the service to assess its usefulness. Any dialogue between the departments and local black communities on the needs of black children was minimal, if at all.

Since the introduction of the Children Act 1989 some research has been undertaken on the general needs of young people leaving care. However, when this interview took place no policies had been formulated by Department B on how it intended to respond to the requirements of the legislation.

The policies of both departments did not stand up well to scrutiny. Although each had equal opportunities policies, there were no strategies for monitoring their practices in relation to matters of ethnicity. Both departments were conscious of the effects this policy vacuum created and the need for staff to be more knowledgeable about racism and its impact on social work practice.

Themes and conclusions

This chapter reiterates some of the common themes that emerge in this study and points to issues that need further exploration. It must be remembered that this is a small qualitative study that offered an opportunity for ten young black people to give voice to their experiences of public care. Consequently, although the findings are of considerable interest and have a validity of their own, no definitive conclusions can be drawn from them regarding local authority practice and service delivery and their impact on young black people. However, much of the experiences recorded in this study echo those in previous ones and it is hoped that they will add to the hitherto limited knowledge base of the experiences of young black children in the care system and leaving care. For the respondents in this study, the principal concerns include a high degree of vulnerability, isolation, loneliness and alienation while in care; poor educational achievements; restricted or no family contact; experience of racism both in the care system and in the school setting; confusion about racial identity; a lack of preparation for transition to adulthood and little after care support.

Preparation for leaving care

In terms of the placement arrangements which were made for the respondents of this study, a correlation was found between placement type and the young people's experiences of leaving care. When they had an opportunity to remain within the extended family and the black community their perception of their black identity was stronger. In this context the young people learned about their "race" and culture and were simultaneously prepared for the transition to adulthood. For one young person who remained in his white extended family, the experience was negative due to several disruptions and changes in placement.

Some who had experienced transracial foster care both in the public and private sectors were not adequately prepared for leaving care; disruptions were common and these had a detrimental effect on continuity of experience. However, those in foster care had a better prognosis than those in residential care, because there were some opportunities to learn some practical skills. Approximately half of the young people studied had an experience of residential care which was negative. They claimed the institutional process had made them more dependent than was desirable, and therefore, less prepared for independence. Regular changes of staff and high numbers of untrained staff militated against understanding the importance of leaving care work and what it entails. The major advantage for those in residential care was the opportunity to meet black staff and black young people with whom they could identify. Undoubtedly this was one of the ways in which important support systems began to develop and led to stronger identity formation.

This study raised many questions about the lack of scholastic achievements and the high incidence of crime. It was striking that in such a small study, six out of ten participants had been permanently excluded from mainstream education, and half the participants had negative contact with the police, three receiving custodial sentences. Poor educational achievement had an impact on the respondents' ability to pursue further studies and/or find employment thereby making a valuable contribution to being self-supporting.

Leaving care work requires a combination of skills development and a continuous process of cultural awareness that should begin from the start of the care experience. Initially, the child is dependent on the care system. However, this should shift to interdependence by developing links between young people and the agencies and services they will be in contact with, for example, housing, social services, educational establishments, and carers and befrienders. In the case of black children, a more integrated and positive approach has to be taken to ensure that "race" and culture are also taken into account and cultural values transmitted. Contingency plans for after care support are necessary as young people are likely to face obstacles after leaving care which make them more vulnerable than the average young person leaving home. Advising young people of their rights and available services after leaving care is crucial in planning for their future. Adequate levels of financial and emotional support should be built into a care plan package. A leaving care model is suggested that requires the following:

1. All local authorities should identify an individual at senior level to be responsible for monitoring and reviewing plans for young people leaving care.

2. All local authorities should set up leaving care and after care teams, with staff who have specialist knowledge of working specifically with young people leaving care, and this work should be prioritised. Disparity between what local authorities offer care leavers should be overcome by the introduction of national standards.

3. Black staff must be recruited at all levels to leaving care and after care teams to ensure that the rights and needs of young black people are addressed.

4. Counselling on matters of "race", culture and identity should be undertaken by specialists with knowledge and experience of working with black children and young people. This service must be offered to all black children in care and should be intensified as part of a leaving care package.

5. Befrienders who can act as appropriate role models should be recruited to support the young person through the leaving care stage and beyond. Such people can also help young black people develop a multiplicity of skills that will give them practical preparation for the transition to adulthood.

6. Black care leavers are also an invaluable resource. They are well equipped to share experiences and help other young black people prepare for leaving care; local authorities should harness their experience.

Most of the young people in this study gave a negative meaning to their care experience and their preparation for leaving care indicating that it was the quality of care that became the main source of their discontent. What became evident was that a system set up and designed to serve the needs of children ultimately failed them, particularly in relation to their racial and cultural needs. Appropriate preparation for leaving care requires more than the teaching of practical skills and the provision of accommodation. It means a commitment to care leavers to meet their needs at all levels and, for black care leavers, to invite and integrate a positive input from black families and from the black community.

Pointers for the future

This study shows that the experiences of young black people in the care system and after care are compounded by their racial and cultural needs at all levels. Although the sample studied is very small, the study paves the way for further research to document and evaluate experience in a number of areas. These include:

- Assessing the educational achievements of black children looked after by the local authority;

- Examining why black young people leaving care are disproportionately over-represented in homelessness and unemployment statistics;

- Evaluating the outcomes of transracial placements and the reasons for the over-representation of African-Caribbean and mixed heritage children in the care system;

- Examining the experiences of young black people who have left care to ascertain what contributes to or hinders progress in the transition to independence;

- Assessing the importance of life skills training and their contribution to leaving care; and

- Considering the experiences of the parents of black children in the care system to establish how best local authorities can work in partnership with them.

Although considerable strides are being made to improve practice and service delivery for young black people in the care system, much of this is patchy and lacks consistency and standards. Below are some pointers that could contribute to the improvement in practice:

- Mechanisms and systems should be developed to ensure that the voices of black children and young people in the care system are heard and that their wishes and feelings are taken into account.

- Local authorities need to use existing legislation more effectively to ensure that "race" and culture are acknowledged as welfare principles.

- Local authorities which are not already practising same-race placements should re-evaluate their significance and recognise the effects of transracial placements on black children with respect to identity development.

- There is an urgent need to expose black children in the care system to black role models – both workers and carers. Black carers should be able to transmit positive values and challenge injustice in an attempt to safeguard the rights of the child.

I've read that they say that you should have coloured people with coloured people, I think that to some extent they should look into that. Coloured people would be able to find their culture and traditions and so on and go to people of their own kind if they have a problem. (Mark)

I think that most black children should be placed with a black family. (Cassie)

What they could have done is vetted the family who adopted me. Placing two black children in a white suburb with a white family was wrong. They could have placed me anywhere with a black family. (David)

- Children who have one parent who is black should not be deprived of having contact with the black parent and their black relatives – they can be crucial in aiding a strong identity development.

- Planning for all children in care is an important aspect of the care process. Integral to planning is looking ahead to the leaving care stage and planning and developing strategies for this.

If social services are not going to provide half-way houses, then find volunteers to come in and talk to them (young people), preferably volunteers who have been through it already. There are plenty of black people out there who have gone through the care system who would most probably be more than willing to help the next lot that are leaving and tell them where to go and where not to go.

If someone was to come and ask me what I think should change in the care system, the first thing I would suggest is find a property that you can break down into bedsits. Stick the kids in while they are still in the children's home. Remove them from the care of the staff and put them in half-way houses. Let them learn how to wash for themselves and cook for themselves. In a children's home all that is done for you. They would have their giros coming into the half-way house and would have to get off their butts and cash their giros, but they would have to balance their money. Unless they have half-way houses, kids that leave care are going to find themselves getting into trouble. I reckon that is why the majority of kids that leave care end up in prison. (Donneth)

If preparation for leaving care is seen as the ultimate goal and if "race" and culture are valued, then preparation for care should dominate the thinking of all staff and carers planning for black children. Effective preparation will only be achieved when a holistic approach is applied. It is only when adults integrate every dimension of caring such as the educational, physical, spiritual, communal, racial and cultural that black young people will be equipped for interacting positively with the outside world. Such preparation will reduce the propensity for discrimination in employment, housing and further education.

Finally, if black young people are to overcome the negative effects of being in care and if they are to become confident, independent young people, they need to be empowered. Empowerment encompasses people's rights, strengths, abilities and encourages the development of their potential. The young black people in this study have spoken movingly and powerfully of their experiences; these testimonies need to be heard and translated into positive action.

I think that social services should still be there when you come out of care. They should teach you the rights and wrongs because when you come out of care you are on your own. I wasn't shown how to live my life. I had to come out of care the hard way, and its very, very hard. (Cassie)